C000178684

Ink and Spirit

Also in the same series:

Seeing Ourselves
   – interpreting contemporary society

   Libby Purves, Robert Blake, Danah
   Zohar & John Habgood

The Retreat of the State
   – nurturing the soul of society

   Nigel Lawson, Arthur Seldon,
   Michael Taylor & David Owen

Ink and Spirit

Literature and Spirituality

Ronald Blythe, Penelope Lively,
Richard Marsh, David Scott
& A. N. Wilson

edited and introduced by
Stephen Platten

CANTERBURY
PRESS
Norwich

© Ronald Blythe, Penelope Lively, Richard Marsh,
Stephen Platten, Davjd Scott & A. N. Wilson 2000

First published in 2000 by The Canterbury Press Norwich
(a publishing imprint of Hymns Ancient & Modern Limited,
a registered charity)
St Mary's Works, St Mary's Plain
Norwich, Norfolk, NR3 3BH

British Library Cataloguing in Publication Data

A catalogue record for this book is available
from the British Library

ISBN 1-85311-363-8

Typeset by Rowland Phototypesetting,
Bury St Edmunds, Suffolk
Printed in Great Britain by
Biddles Ltd, Guildford and King's Lynn

Contents

Contributors

Ronald Blythe, novelist, essayist and biographer, is the author of numerous publications including *Akenfield*, *First Friends*, *Divine Landscapes* and *Word from Wormingford*.

Penelope Lively was awarded the Booker Prize in 1987 for *Moon Tiger* and the Carnegie Medal for her children's novel, *The Ghost of Thomas Kempe* in 1973.

Richard Marsh is the Archbishop of Canterbury's Secretary for Ecumenical Affairs.

Stephen Platten is Dean of Norwich.

David Scott is a parish priest and poet. He is Warden of Spirituality in the Diocese of Winchester.

A. N. Wilson is a novelist, journalist and literary critic.

Preface

This book brings together in an edited form four essays which were originally delivered as the third series of Launcelot Fleming Lectures sponsored jointly by Norwich Cathedral and the University of East Anglia in the autumn of 1999.

Launcelot Fleming was Bishop of Norwich from 1959 to 1971. During that time he worked hard to forge a strong and productive relationship between the Church and the newly founded University. His broad sympathies, his Christian humanism and his background of wide interests ranging from Antarctic exploration to leadership in the Church during a time of radical change, were the reasons why this annual set of lectures was dedicated to his name. Our aim is to choose subjects where Church, theology and society engage with each other.

The inter-relationship between literature and the Christian tradition is almost as long as the history of that tradition itself. In the past two centuries, with rapid changes in the cultural background, the inter-relationship between literature and spirituality has become ever more interesting and complex. These essays seek to address these issues from different points of view, including people who are both believers and non-believers. I have introduced them with an extended reflection on the wider background to Christianity and imaginative literature, and Ronald Blythe kindly supplied a fascinating and stimulating final reflection.

Stephen Platten
Norwich
June 2000

Introduction: Ink Tempered with Love

STEPHEN PLATTEN

Narrative in Religion and Philosophy

> And when Love speaks, the voice of all the gods
> Makes heaven drowsy with the harmony,
> Never durst poet touch a pen to write
> Until his ink were tempered with Love's sighs.[1]

If ink being 'tempered with Love' means poetry and prose acting as vehicles for the transmission of the fears and aspirations of the human spirit, then this mood has surely been with literature from the start. The twin peaks of Mount Parnassus were dedicated to Apollo with the Muses and to Dionysius; literature was the vehicle then that spoke not only of the human spirit, but also of how that spirit was caught up into the world of the gods. Tragedy, comedy and reflection upon the nature of human existence were expressed through narrative, poetry and drama. The philosophy of Plato is itself rehearsed in the form of dialogues; such dialogues may seem to be rather forced as pieces of drama, but still the form gives shape and energy to the patterns of human philosophizing and contemplation. Similarly some of the pre-Socratic philosophers, such as Parmenides and Empedocles, clothed their philosophical ideas in poetry.

The Judaeo–Christian tradition also uses literary media to communicate those things that are critical to the human spirit and to humanity's attempts to conceptualize relationships with God. The lives of Abraham, Isaac, Jacob and the other patriarchs, together with the vicissitudes of the growth of the Israelite nation, are all clothed in narrative. But these narratives are never simply naïve tales – instead, either on the surface or woven into the text are lessons for all time. The stories of Adam and Eve and of Cain and Abel seek to tell of the origins of good and evil; indeed, later generations often read off rather too crudely the implications of these symbolic narratives for their own age. The writings of the 'deuteronomic historian' in Joshua, Judges, 1 and 2 Samuel and 1 and 2 Kings equally wove a fairly explicit moralism into the fabric of the narrative. Israel suffered because the nation had done what was evil in the sight of the Lord; Jezebel's foreign gods and the apostasy which they caused had dramatic results for the vulnerable Jewish nation, placed perilously as it was between the vying power blocs of the ancient world.

It is not only narrative, however, that has modulated the divine voice for the human auditor. Poetry, too, is a medium that has, to some degree, been partially fashioned by biblical patterns and examples. The Psalter – by turns the hymnbook, the prayer manual and the source of consolation for the Jewish people – is taken into the heart of the Christian tradition; it is words from Psalm 22:1 that are recorded on the lips of Jesus just before he breathes his last: 'My God, my God, why hast thou forsaken me?' In the Old Testament we also find love poetry of the most erotic form in the *Song of Songs*, and in the 'Wisdom literature', the inspired reflections of Job on humanity and the problem of evil, as well as the world-weary reflections of Qoheleth, or the 'Preacher', as he calls himself in the book of Ecclesiastes. Indeed, throughout the literature of the Bible there are encapsulated nuggets of poetry in both the Old and New Testaments. The Bible is dominated by the use of images whether in poetry or prose; history and imagery are combined, as Erich Auerbach indicates in his great analysis of the representation of reality in Western literature.[2]

I shall return to this theme of the use of the figural imagination for the transmission of religious ideas and beliefs towards the conclusion of this introduction. It is an essential theme in any attempt to understand both the nature of religious language, and the means by which texts which are claimed to be revelatory transmit divine truth. The relationship between religion and literature is, however, reciprocal. For not only is literary imagery used to convey religious truth, but imaginative literary texts themselves often reflect religious themes and struggle to engage with meaning and destiny within human life. If one combines these insights then the relationship between religion and literature becomes subtle, complex and multi-layered. The richness of this intersection cannot be exaggerated.

3

It is a commonplace to note that not only in the world of visual art, but also in the realm of imaginative litera- ture, the reservoir of biblical narrative and poetry has been drawn upon by countless novelists throughout the past two centuries; a frequent focus for study and a rich seam for those who would dig for doctoral theses has been in the impact of the Bible upon individual writers. The origins of modern fiction are frequently traced to the eighteenth century, and notably to the writings of Henry Fielding. Virtually from the beginning the novel has been encrusted with images and narrative material that find their roots in the literature of the Old and New Testaments; certainly there are numerous examples of this, for example, in the novels of Sir Walter Scott. Ironi- cally during this same period, however, another force was at work which has led to a tension between religion – notably Christianity – and imaginative literature. That force is the growth of critical scholarly techniques, born of what we know now as the Enlightenment.

These techniques have subjected both biblical narra- tive and religious belief to scrutiny. The twin disciplines of historical and literary criticism have suggested that the process whereby the books of the Bible have come into being is lengthy and complex. The Pentateuch – the first five books of the Old Testament – is probably the edited compilation of a number of discrete sources. Using a not dissimilar literary technique, the first three Synoptic Gospels can be placed alongside each other to reveal a process of development and 'redaction' or edit- ing by successive evangelists. Mark is believed to be the earliest Gospel and Matthew and Luke, it is argued, use

Mark as their main source and add to it other material from their own communities.

The irony then, is that as the art of novel-writing developed, so Christian images were almost relentlessly pressed into service with the attendant weaving of the Bible into this new cultural form, and yet at the very same time a different literary process, rooted in critical techniques, began to undermine the confidence of scholars in the biblical documents as sources of divine revelation. The Bible became an essential source for contemporary literature; literary criticism relativized biblical authority.

The Rise of Scepticism

Understandably, then, this set of critical techniques led people to interpret the biblical texts in a rather different light. Harmonization has become unfashionable and the Bible is now seen as a library of varied books dating from a period of almost 1000 years, if one includes the oral traditions which stand behind the written text. Alongside this the Enlightenment brought with it further corrosive elements, notably in the realm of philosophy. Alasdair MacIntyre has argued that until the Enlightenment, Western philosophy had largely been viewed as an 'additive' process. The Aristotelian tradition had dominated and St Thomas Aquinas had helped consolidate this from the point of view of Christian theology.[3] The rise of empirical and sceptical philosophy with the work of John Locke and David Hume, and also the influential writings of Immanuel Kant, all led to a more

fragmented scene. Furthermore, the growth of scepticism itself contributed to the critical momentum which
was gathering apace. The optimistic philosophy of Gott-
fried Leibniz, which proclaimed that our world is 'the
best of all possible worlds', was parodied by Voltaire
in his *Candide* which responded to the tragedy of the
Lisbon earthquake of 1755. Voltaire's work in some
ways marks the earliest example of such religious scepticism in a significant piece of imaginative literature. This
set the scene for some of the developments of the following century. In the field of the novel, for example, George
Eliot was a religious sceptic. Among other things she
translated one of the most radical literary-critical essays
on the Christian faith, namely D. F. Strauss's *The Life
of Jesus Critically Examined*.[4]

It would, however, be a mistake to characterize the
eighteenth and nineteenth centuries as a period in which
there was an uninterrupted rise in the sceptical literary
impulse. Indeed, some writers demonstrated remarkable
and positive innovation in the realm of religious
thought. Pre-eminent among these was Samuel Taylor
Coleridge, who argued that there was no inherent oppo-
sition between religious belief and the development of
modern science and the critical method. While being
strongly affected by the contemporary philosophical
trends, Coleridge engaged positively with these chal-
lenges to argue for a philosophy of religion that
embraced this critical approach. His poetry often
breathes a strong religious atmosphere and brings a
quasi-mystical feeling with it which should not be put
down merely to the influence of opium. In his later writ-

ings, and notably in *The Everlasting Gospel*, William Blake, effectively a contemporary, shows similar tendencies towards an undogmatic and all-embracing mystical religious approach. Other writers were more orthodox in their religious response. This is notably true in the poetic writings of John Henry Newman and Gerard Manley Hopkins, both of whom later became converts to Roman Catholicism.

Alongside these writers, however, there arose a broader, more uncertain tide within Victorian literature. This is often focused in Matthew Arnold's celebrated poem 'Dover Beach', which is seen as crystallizing the religious uncertainties inherent in later Victorian intellectual circles:

The Sea of Faith
Was once, too, at the full, and round earth's shore
Lay like the folds of a bright girdle furled.
But now I only hear
Its melancholy, long, withdrawing roar,
Retreating to the breath
Of the night-wind, down the vast edges drear
And naked shingles of the world.[5]

Arnold's poetry is too easily identified with an outright rejection of Christian belief which captures neither the spirit of the age nor the instincts of Arnold himself which were towards an 'ethical' appreciation of religious belief rooted in the Old Testament and refracted through the personal teaching of Jesus; Christianity for him became 'morality touched by emotion'.[6] Similar chords resonated in the life and work of Arnold's tragic friend, Arthur Hugh Clough, whose personality had partially been crushed through the powerful influence of his headmaster, Thomas Arnold (Matthew's father). Clough, too, had a crisis of faith which is scarcely concealed in the semi-cynical mood of some of his poetry. It is there in 'The Latest Decalogue':

> Thou shalt not kill, but need'st not strive
> Officiously to keep alive:
> Do not adultery commit;
> Advantage rarely comes of it.[7]

It is even more prominent in 'There is No God':

> 'There is no God,' the wicked saith,
>   'And truly it's a blessing,
> For what he might have done with us
>   It's better only guessing'
> . . .
> almost everyone when age,
>   Disease or sorrow strike him,
> Inclines to think there is a God,
>   Or something very like him.[8]

Tennyson's Agonies

Other nineteenth-century poets are still more agonized in the manner in which they deal with their uncertainties. Alfred Lord Tennyson is often seem as the paradigm poet of the Victorian age, and his engagement with faith and doubt as a classical expression of an age of religious uncertainty. In Tennyson it is focused particularly by the loss of his friend Arthur Hallam in his untimely death at the age of 22. Much of his writing is dominated by Hallam's death and this experience is exacerbated by the instability of Tennyson's own background: his father was plagued by depression, epilepsy, and drug and alcohol addiction. Tennyson himself was a hypochondriac and sensitive to every change of mood. It is in his 'In Memoriam' that Tennyson's response to Hallam's death is most sharply drawn with regard to religious experience:

> I falter where I firmly trod,
>   And falling with my weight of cares
>   Upon the world's great altar stairs
> That slope through darkness up to God,
>
> I stretch lame hands of faith, and grope,
>   And gather dust and chaff and call
>   To what I feel is Lord of all,
> And faintly trust the larger hope.[9]

Even nature appears to be callous and wasteful:

> Are God and Nature then at strife,
>   That nature lends such evil dreams?
>   So careful of the type she seems,
> So careless of the single life.[10]

Here, of course, Tennyson is tangling with issues which would dominate the intellectual community in the mid-nineteenth century with the publication of Darwin's *The Origin of Species* and with the work of T. H. Huxley and others. Here imaginative writing, then, is reflecting a wider set of uncertainties. It was also Tennyson, in 'In Memoriam', who would coin the phrase 'Nature, red in tooth and claw'. Tennyson, however, characterizes the wavering and undogmatic spirit of his times, since often he will surge back into a more optimistic mood. In 'In Memoriam', towards the end, the mood moves onto a more positive assertion of faith:

> Ring in the valiant man and free,
> The larger heart, the kindlier hand;
> Ring out the darkness of the land,
> Ring in the Christ that is to be.[11]

And then in the final stanza:

> That God, which ever lives and loves,
> One God, one law, one element,
> And one far-off divine event,
> To which the whole creation moves.[12]

Here Tennyson pre-empts something of the eschatological optimism of theological writers of the early twentieth century, and particularly the writings of the Jesuit, Teilhard de Chardin. This spirit in Tennyson seems ultimately to triumph over his abiding gloom and nowhere more so than in the sentimental lines which he wrote when making his way home to Farringford, crossing to the Isle of Wight from Lymington to Yarmouth. He insisted that these lines should always conclude his collected works:

> For tho' from out of bourne of Time and Place
> The flood may bear me far
> I hope to see my Pilot face to face
> When I have crost the bar.[13]

Hardy and Faith

This veiled optimism is mirrored by a veiled pessimism in some of the greatest poems of Thomas Hardy. Hardy is effectively one generation on from Tennyson and he bridges the centuries while remaining in essence a Victorian voice. Despite this, Hardy, both in his novels and in his poetry, is aware that he stands at a crossroads or on the threshold of what we would now call modernity. Written on the very eve of the new century, Hardy muses, for example, upon a moth, a long-legs and a dumble-dore (bumble bee) flying around his lamp. So he concludes:

> My guests besmear my new-penned line,
> Or bang at the lamp and fall supine.
> 'God's humblest, they!' I muse. Yet why?
> They know Earth-secrets that know not I.[14]

In his novels, too, Hardy struggles with a number of themes which gnaw away at any certain faith. The rural scene is invaded by the machinery of a more rapacious age; the snobbery of the class system puts down even the most talented; the coldness of the established Church hardly speaks of an all-loving God. Hardy's observance of the tragic nature of certain aspects of human life further increase his scepticism. Hardy's uncertainty, even bleakness, are perhaps classically expressed in his poem 'The Darkling Thrush':

> So little cause for carolings
>   Of such ecstatic sound
> Was written on terrestrial things
>   Afar or nigh around,
> That I could think there trembled through
>   His happy good-night air
> Some blessed Hope, whereof he knew
>   And I was unaware.[15]

The writings of Hardy, Tennyson and a number of other Victorian poets suggest a real seeking after meaning in something of the manner in which Penelope Lively suggests fiction may strive to seek an order or at least a means of ordering our existence. Certainly a careful reflection upon Hardy's life suggests that the picture sometimes painted of a cynical atheistic approach to the universe is far too crude and unsophisticated when compared with the facts. Despite his uncertainties, Hardy seems to have continued to search even up until the final years of his life. In extreme old age he continued to cross the fields from his house, Max Gate, outside

Dorchester to attend evensong at Stinsford, the church in whose choir he had sung as a child.

In a fascinating passage which is part of the *Apology* (introduction) to his collection of poems *Late Lyrics and Earlier* of 1922, he writes:

> In any event poetry, pure literature in general, and religion – I include religion, in its essential and undogmatic sense, because poetry and religion touch each other, or rather modulate into each other, are indeed, often but different names for the same thing . . .

Later he continues:

> For since the historic and once august hierarchy of Rome some generations ago lost its chance of being the religion of the future by doing otherwise and throwing over a little band of New Catholics who were making a struggle for continuity by applying the principle of evolution to their own faith . . . since, then, one may ask, what other purely English establishment than the Church, of sufficient dignity and footing, with such strength of old association, such scope for transmutability, such architectural spell, is left in this country to keep the shreds of morality together.[16]

This 'little band of New Catholics' is precisely that group of Roman Catholic modernists referred to by A. N. Wilson in his essay, where he also laments their demise on account of the defensiveness of the Church.

Wilson, too, seems to retain a wistful hope that the Church might offer something to this generation. Despite Hardy's uncertainty, then, which is reinforced in a footnote to the above quotation which argues that 'one must not be too sanguine in reading the signs', still he presses the claims of religion, for in the next sentence he asserts:

> It may indeed be a forlorn hope, a mere dream, that of an alliance between religion, which must be retained unless the world is to perish, and complete rationality, which must come, unless also the world is to perish, by means of the interfusing effect of poetry . . .[17]

One can see Hardy's reflections here as a continuation of his lifelong struggle which began with thoughts of ordination and continued with some of the tragic reflections within his novels. Sometimes this tragic metaphysic is played out at the subliminal level, for example, in Clym Yeobright's increasing blindness (*The Return of the Native*), in Michael Henchard's moral torpor (*The Mayor of Casterbridge*); on other occasions he is more explicit, as in his reference to the 'President of the Immortals ending his sport with Tess', at the end of *Tess of the D'Urbervilles*. This interplay reflects some of the themes explored by Penelope Lively in her discussion of religion and the rise of fiction. Hardy is, of course, but one case in point and a very particular case at that. Nevertheless his fiction was being written against the canvas of increasing uncertainty and scepticism in the last quarter of the nineteenth century.

Introduction: Ink Tempered with Love

The End of Innocence

Within the first quarter of the twentieth century there was a further dramatic cultural shift which no one could have predicted. This shift was the product of the First World War, a catastrophe of tragic proportions for the human race.

> Never such innocence,
> Never before or since,
> As changed itself to past
> Without a word – the men
> Leaving the gardens tidy,
> The thousands of marriages
> Lasting a little while longer:
> Never such innocence again.[18]

These lines, the last stanza of Philip Larkin's poem '*MCMXIV*', capture poignantly the seminal changes wrought by the Great War upon Western culture. Alongside the increasing religious uncertainty of the nineteenth century (and to some extent fuelling it) came enormous strides in scientific research; this was itself paralleled by an advancing sense of progress and optimism within the human community marked, for example, in the writings of Herbert Spencer and others. These writings simply traced the contours of a wider sense of progress which was further fed by the industrial success of many Western nations and by the feeling that some of the deeper problems facing humanity were on the verge of being solved; advances in medical science supported such a changing attitude of mind.

In the face of all this, the outbreak of war in 1914 initially could be approached with confidence and even with some feeling of the romance of gallantry. Rupert Brooke's well-known lines succinctly crystallize such a mood:

> If I should die, think only this of me:
>> That there's some corner of a foreign field
> That is for ever England.
> . . .
> And think, this heart, all evil shed away,
>> A pulse in the eternal mind, no less
>>> Gives somewhere back the thoughts by
>>>> England given[19]

All evil, however, could not be shed away and as the full horror of the war in Flanders unfolded so the hopes of a complete generation were shattered by the shell-shock and liquid mud of Ypres, the Somme and Passchendaele. The events of the First World War – particularly the waste of young humanity combined with an increasing sense of the meaninglessness of the carnage and thus an uncertainty about the reasons for fighting – refocused the mood of Western culture. It was as if all experience, both individual and communal, had been passed through an enormous lens which would refract patterns in a manner that would spell a permanent change in cultural mood. Talk of human progress now seemed shallow in the face of such suffering and in the light of such a significant failure of civilization. Optimism fell victim to an advancing feeling of futility.

Introduction: Ink Tempered with Love

The liberal theology which had characterized much Protestant thought (and which had even flowered momentarily in Roman Catholicism, within that small group of theological modernists) gave way to a new orthodoxy underpinned by a pervading pessimism about human nature. Karl Barth, the seminal Swiss Calvinist theologian, set up a scaffolding upon which even more liberal voices, such as the American theologian Reinhold Niebuhr, would find themselves constrained to build. It was the refocusing effects of the Great War that had concentrated people's minds. The lens that allowed such refocusing projected its images most sharply in the artistic fruits of the war. Paul Nash's paintings of the trenches and the blighted fields of Flanders were matched by the harsh and brutal realism of the poetry and prose which issued from the war. In a classic study of the changes wrought in literature, Paul Fussell wrote:

> The image of strict division dominates the Great War conception of Time Before and Time After, especially when the mind dwells on the contrast between the pre-war idyll and the wartime nastiness.[20]

This nastiness was depicted on countless occasions by the remarkable poets, playwrights and prose authors born of and fascinated by the conflict. The poetic output of the war was extraordinary. Often the literary imagery and expression used by these writers picks up clear religious resonances, albeit on many occasions couched in angry and defiant words. A poem which somehow brings together the entire panorama of the Great War and its effect upon European culture is Wilfred Owen's 'Parable of the Old Man and the Young':

> Then Abram bound the youth with belts and straps,
> And builded parapets and trenches there,
> And stretched forth the knife to slay his son.
> When lo! an angel called him out of heaven,
> Saying, Lay not thy hand upon the lad,
> Neither do anything to him. Behold,
> A ram, caught in a thicket by its horns;
> Offer the Ram of Pride instead of him.
> But the old man would not so, but slew his son,
> And half the seed of Europe, one by one.[21]

Time and again religious images are used which often showed themselves to rebel against the past and against the meaninglessness of war. In 'Dead Man's Dump', Isaac Rosenberg wrote:

> What fierce imaginings their dark souls lit!
> Earth! Have they gone into you?
> Somewhere they must have gone
> And flung on your hard back
> Is their soul's sack
> Emptied of God – ancestralled essences.
> Who hurled them out? Who hurled?[22]

Countless examples could be given of poetry protesting against conflict and premature death. Such literature also began to explore the manner in which the corporate experience of the First World War changed and purged

Western culture. It was not just the poetry of the war itself which expressed such change. The literature that followed mirrored this change and perhaps none so sharply as T. S. Eliot's *The Waste Land*, written immediately after the Great War and depicting a wilderness with scant grounds for hope and the fragmentation of culture into forms of uncertainty and unbelief.

Looking Before and After

As Richard Marsh indicates in his essay, however, from the carnage and destruction came also a more positive attempt to recapture and revivify images from the Judaeo–Christian tradition. The process of anamnesis, a term coined by Plato meaning a remembering or re-learning of the past, was reborn in the early Christian Church in a manner which also paid tribute to the Jewish Passover tradition. Plato's pattern of anamnesis underpinned a theory of knowledge that saw the quest for truth as a rediscovery, a remembering of the world out of which we were born – all learning was a remembering. The Jewish remembering at Passover was more dynamic. Each Passover Feast not only remembered the events in Egypt, but in doing so again made available the salvation first given by God. In the Christian Eucharist, the Mass, this same tradition promises present grace through the performance of the sacrament. Here lies the heart of the imagery in David Jones's later work *The Anathemata*. In his earlier work, *In Parenthesis*, which issued more directly from his experiences in the Great War, memories which can be so destructive and paralysing are the vehicles for the refashioning of experience, both individually and in community. Jones returned from the war with his faith articulated rather than destroyed.

Despite the rise of secularism and the increased marginalization of religion, literature and religious experience continue to be intertwined and to feed each other. In his trenchantly critical essay, A. N. Wilson reminds us of the nourishing poetry of the later Eliot and notably in *The Four Quartets*. Here the tradition is ransacked over and over again for imagery which dances on the edge of contemplation. The poetry of Edwin Muir similarly is constructive in its combination of imagery and religious experience. Indeed, in a famous poem, Muir aggressively asserts the power of imagery in religion which takes us beyond the verbal into the personal imagery which remains central to Christianity:

> The Word made flesh here is made word again,
> A word made word in flourish and arrogant crook.
> See there King Calvin with his iron pen,
> And God three angry letters in a book,[23]

Eliot, Muir and others continue the tradition of Christian poetry that David Scott alludes to so lyrically in his essay. Scott makes it clear that such a tradition includes those of which he himself is a living example, the parson poet. It is a tradition that has been ascetically nourished in the writings of R. S. Thomas. Thomas, too, reflects upon that tradition which ultimately leaves words behind and moves towards the negation of images. It is a tradition of the desert which accepts the need to live with an aridity and an absence of God:

> There is no other sound
> In the darkness but the sound of a man
> Breathing, testing his faith
> On emptiness, nailing his questions
> One by one to an untenanted cross.[24]

It ought not to be too surprising that the tradition of the parson-poet has survived or even thrives into this relatively harsh un-religious climate at the beginning of the third millennium. For at the heart of the Christian faith ineluctably stands the central place of imagery. This introduction has focused mainly upon poetry, but throughout the biblical tradition with which I began one encounters the central role of imagery. Often images are clothed in narrative, and the promise of salvation is dramatically acted out by human figures in whose activity can be discerned the grace of God. The pilgrim people of Israel are saved more than once and this narrative imagery has retained its power for over two millennia: the passage through the Red Sea on dry land, the saving grace offered at the Passover and the establishment of the Davidic Kingdom are but three images which are controlling figural patterns in the Old Testament. In the New Testament, the image of incarnation, variously described in the birth stories of the Gospels and the mystery theology of John 1, stands alongside the other powerful imagery of redemption in the cross. That crucifixion imagery itself is variously described by the evangelists and by Paul. Often the New Testament re-pristinates the imagery of the Old: baptism becomes a new crossing of the Red Sea; the Sermon on the Mount is almost a figural repetition of the Pentateuch, of the Torah – Jesus does not come to destroy the law and the prophets but to fulfil them (Matthew 5:17). Indeed this teaching is set out within five great antitheses which refer back to the Pentateuch and seek to correct some of the corruptions (as Matthew's Gospel sees it) in the Jewish oral tradition.[25]

The means by which religious truth is communicated in the biblical texts cannot be understood without an understanding of literary imagery. In one of the most original and sophisticated treatments of biblical interpretation of the last half of the twentieth century, Austin Farrer writes:

> I would dare to think that sometimes my thought would become diaphanous, so that there should be some perception of the divine cause shining through the created effect, as a deep pool, settling into a clear tranquillity, permits us to see the spring in the bottom of it from which its waters rise.[26]

This is nothing less than a description of the manner in which the Bible communicates religious truth; it is in a succession of controlling images. It is no accident that Farrer was both a biblical and a philosophical theo-logian, for Christian doctrine is itself only communicable through image and analogy. Much of the process of theological discourse consists of a sophisticated critique of images in order better to appreciate something of the nature of God and of God's relationship to humanity.

This suggests that the communication of religious truths in the Bible, in the later tradition and in contemporary theological discourse, is not discontinuous. Throughout, the theologian, the pastor and the preacher are challenged to communicate the things of God through the use of imagery and the criticism of images. Preaching is itself a further development of this same literary process and use of images. In one of the richest reflections on the art of preaching, R. E. C. Browne wrote:

> Perhaps all who write great poetry are carried into the realms of religion whether they know it or not, but it is certainly true that the attempt to express religious truths carries a man into the realm of poetry whether he knows it or not.[27]

If this is the case, then we can understand something of the tension, of the uncertainties and of the richness in the areas which this book seeks to explore. The religious explorer can hardly avoid the realm of literature and the parson-poet is one example of this. Development of the tradition will, however, require debate, disputation and even an evolution of theological thought. Against this canvas people will always stand variously on either side of the divide between belief and agnosticism. Among modern novelists, Graham Greene and Iris Murdoch are examples of two writers who stood on opposite sides of this divide, but in each case perhaps only just. Meanwhile both within and outside the community of faith the quest continues, the images multiply and the narrative moves on. The ink continues to be tempered with love's sighs.

Notes

1. William Shakespeare, *Love's Labour Lost*, Act 4, Scene 3.
2. Erich Auerbach, *Mimesis* (Princeton, NJ: Princeton University Press, 1953). See especially his comments on 'figural interpretation' (pp. 73, 48–49).
3. Alasdair MacIntyre, *After Virtue* (Duckworth, London, 1981).
4. David Friedrich Strauss in Peter Hodgson (ed.), *The Life of Jesus Critically Examined* (London: SCM Press, 1973).
5. Matthew Arnold, 'Dover Beach', in *The New Oxford Book of English Verse* (London: Oxford University Press, 1972), p. 703.
6. Matthew Arnold, *Literature and Dogma* (1873), chapter 1.
7. A. H. Clough, 'The Latest Decalogue', in *English Verse*, p. 682.
8. A. H. Clough, 'There is No God', in *English Verse*, pp. 684–85.
9. Alfred Tennyson, 'In Memoriam', in his *Poems and Plays* (Oxford: Oxford University Press, 1965), p. 243.
10. Tennyson, 'In Memoriam', p. 243.
11. Tennyson, 'In Memoriam', p. 258.
12. Tennyson, 'In Memoriam', p. 266.
13. Tennyson, 'Crossing the Bar', in *Poems and Plays*, p. 831.
14. Thomas Hardy, 'An August Midnight', in his *Collected Poems* (London: Macmillan, 1976), p. 146.
15. Thomas Hardy, 'The Darkling Thrush', in *Collected Poems*, p. 150.
16. Hardy, *Collected Poems*, p. 561.
17. Hardy, *Collected Poems*, pp. 561–62.
18. Philip Larkin, 'MCMXIV', in his *Collected Poems* (London: Faber & Faber, 1988), pp. 127–28.

Introduction: Ink Tempered with Love

19. Rupert Brooke, 'The Soldier', in *English Verse*, p. 863.
20. Paul Fussell, *The Great War and Modern Memory* (London: Oxford University Press, 1975), p. 80.
21. Wilfred Owen, 'Parable of the Old Man and the Young', in his *Collected Poems* (London: Chatto & Windus, 1963), p. 42.
22. Isaac Rosenberg, 'Dead Man's Dump', in Martin Stephen, *Never Such Innocence* (London: Buchan and Enright, 1988), p. 155.
23. Edwin Muir, 'The Incarnate One', in his *Collected Poems* (London: Faber & Faber, 1960), p. 228.
24. R. S. Thomas, 'In Church', in his *Selected Poems* (London: Granada, 1979), p. 104.
25. See, e.g., H. Benedict Green, *The Gospel According to St Matthew* (Oxford: Oxford University Press, 1975), pp. 16ff., 81ff.; and W. D. Davies, *The Sermon on the Mount* (Cambridge: Cambridge University Press, 1966), pp. 6ff.
26. Austin Farrer, *The Glass of Vision* (London: Dacre Press, 1948), p. 8.
27. R. E. C. Browne, *The Ministry of the Word* (London: SCM Press, 1976), p. 31.

Religion, Literature and the Third Millennium

DAVID SCOTT

Poetry in the Making

I begin with a story many people will know from Bede's *Ecclesiastical History of the English People*:

> In the monastery of Streanaeschalch, (pronounced, I believe, Whitby, by the locals) lived a brother singularly gifted by God's grace . . . It sometimes happened at a feast that all the guests in turn would be invited to sing and entertain the company; [but] one evening this brother, seeing the harp coming his way, got up from the table and went out to the stable where it was his duty to look after the beasts. Then, when the time came he settled down to sleep.
>
> Suddenly, in a dream he saw a man standing beside him who called him by name. 'Caedmon,' he said, 'sing me a song.'
>
> 'I don't know how to sing,' Caedmon replied. 'It is because I cannot sing that I left the feast and came here.'

The man who addressed him then said: 'But you shall sing to me.'

'What should I sing about?' he replied.

'Sing about the creation of all things,' the other answered.

And Caedmon immediately began to sing verses in praise of God the creator that he had never heard before, and their theme ran thus:

Now hail we the maker	of heaven's wide fabric
Majesty's might	his miracle mind
Work of the world warden	worker of wonders
Now he, the Lord,	of glory eternal
He made for mankind	heaven the barn-roof
Middle-earth also	mankind's ward.[1]

That poem, considered to be the first poem in English, came top of the 100 millennium 'Poems on the Underground' commissioned by London Transport. (If you're lucky you'll catch it on the Circle Line in the rush hour, but you might have to ask someone to move their head for you to read it all!)

I have a theory that Caedmon had fallen in love with something or somebody, and not being able to cope with the hearties, scoffing the wassail out of bulls' horns and singing the Saxon equivalent of rugby songs, went out to the place he felt happier – the barn. He had fallen in love with the gospel, and he only needed that voice in the barn to encourage him to dig out his poetry from what was dearest but most secret to his heart. That time in the barn was a moment of revelation every bit as dramatic as the prodigal son coming to himself in the pigsty; as Mary giving birth in the stable; as Dylan Thomas's 'in the blind barns and byres of the windless farm';[2] and as David Jones peeping through the crack in the old farm building in the First World War to see Mass being celebrated by 'a sacerdos in a gilt hued planeta' and two or three huddled figures in khaki.[3] 'Sing Caedmon, about the creation of all things. Sing about what you know, the gift you have been given by the Holy Spirit of God.' So the first point I want to emphasize is this: deep within some people in each generation of the Church is the gift of a song or poem, waiting to be called out by the voice in the barn, usually at some distance from the party.

Early in the morning, Caedmon went to his superior, the Reeve, and told him about this gift that he had received. The Reeve took him before the Abbess (Hilda), who ordered him to give an account of his dream and repeat the verses in the presence of many learned men, so that a decision might be reached by common consent as to their quality and origin. All of them agreed that Caedmon's gift had been given him by the Lord. I shall look at that gift a little closer, since I'm a great believer in things coming in from outside. I suppose 'the muse landing' is a similar way of putting it, though the muse can come in a very prosaic form. This was the way it came to me.

The Impulse to Write

It was the early 1960s and I was at boarding school from the time when I couldn't see any of the mirrors without standing on a stool, to the day that the Beatles released 'Father Mackenzie, darning his socks and writing his sermons that no one will hear' ('Eleanor Rigby'). We had a housematron, and most of that time the matron was the same Welsh lady, who was given the honourable title of 'The Old Grey Mare'. It came to the day when she was to leave, and it was decided to give her a gift, and for a small speech to be made. Who was to make the speech? They asked me. I was given about an hour's notice to write this piece of formal flattery, in English (for gone were the days at Dimwash College when you formalized superlatives in the 'issimas' of Latin, and the 'megas' of Greek). I reminded her of the supreme skill she had shown in deciding which of the two giant bottles of coloured water to pour into the spoon for all symptoms: broken legs, diarrhoea, bedwetting, impetigo and just plain skiving. I thanked her for, well, just being her. She was well pleased and so was I at being able to produce the goods, under pressure, in the words required. That was all to do with the gift somehow landing in the form of a request. I didn't know I could do that sort of thing until I was asked. I can't even remember now who asked me, but ask they did, and I set to. It revealed something in me that I didn't think I had, that was not in the first place of my choosing, but was work to order – a commission, called out from the needs of the community. Therefore, my second point is this: poetry often needs a midwife. The Church could be more of a midwife to poetry, as it was for Caedmon. By the Church, I mean the community of Christians, be it a parish, a school, a cathedral, a base community in South America or a religious community in New Zealand. We should all be on the look out.

Another, rather more significant and anguished, example of the Church prompting poetry, and then getting cold feet, brings us to that great religious poet, Father Gerard Manley Hopkins SJ (1844–89). When Hopkins entered the Jesuit noviciate at Manresa House in Roehampton, he felt it incumbent on him to stop writing poems. I suppose he thought they were too self-indulgent, too much open to pride, and a distraction from the core syllabus of Ignatian Exercises and poor food. Yet he did write several poems to order, for the festivals of the Blessed Virgin Mary (these were hung around the necks of the statues, and – no doubt pre-Vatican II – they were spoilt for choice as to which one to use). One afternoon a few years later, this time at St Beuno's in North Wales, when the rhythms of the Welsh landscape and traditional Welsh poetic form of 'cynganaed' were filling his head, his Rector, Father Jones, set in motion one of the great renewals of religious poetry. Hopkins writes about that moment, rather matter-of-factly, to his Anglican friend, historian and poet, Canon R. W. Dixon:

> You ask, do I write verse myself. What I had written I burnt before I became a Jesuit and resolved to write no more, as not belonging to my profession, unless it

were by the wish of my superiors; so for seven years I wrote nothing but two or three little presentation pieces which occasion called for. But when in the winter of '75 the Deutschland was wrecked in the mouth of the Thames and five Franciscan nuns, exiles from Germany by the Falck Laws, aboard of her were drowned I was affected by the account and happened to say so to my rector, he said that he wished someone would write a poem on the subject. On this hint I set to work and, though my hand was out at first, produced one.[4]

> Thou mastering me
> God! Giver of breath and bread;
> World's strand, sway of the sea;
> Lord of living and dead;
> Thou has bound bones and veins in me, fastened
>   me flesh,
> And after it almost unmade, what with dread,
>   Thy doing: and dost thou touch me afresh?
> Over again I feel the finger and find thee.[5]

Good for the Rector, I say. 'Hopkins, sing me a song.' The request, I want to emphasize, came from the rector of the community at St Beuno's. Hopkins wrote the poem, 'by the wish of his superior'. Here was a providential coming together of a subject, a poet, a rhythm and a request. So Hopkins set to.

The sad history of the non-publication of 'The Wreck of the Deutschland' is quite another matter. Hopkins submitted the completed poem to the editor of the Jesuit

David Scott

periodical *The Month*, and the editor couldn't make head nor tail of it. It wasn't published, nor were any other of Hopkins's poems in his lifetime (I don't think, after the disappointment of 'The Wreck', Hopkins wanted them to be published). It was Hopkins's friend Robert Bridges, the Poet Laureate, who published a selection of the poems in his wartime anthology *The Spirit of Man*, and this brought the name of Hopkins to people's attention. The Church of Hopkins's time could find no place for his poems in its publications, nor in its liturgy, nor in the general circulation of Catholic poetry. Their time was not yet. Hopkins died with the words 'I am very happy' on his lips, but his poems were not known, and his later years were ones of intense frustration and anguish. He wrote what are referred to as the 'Terrible Sonnets':

'To seem the stranger lies my lot, my life among strangers.'[6]

'I wake and feel the fell of dark, not day.'[7]

'No worst, there is none. Pitched past pitch of grief.'[8]

If we see Caedmon as representing the poet who, within the Christian community he belonged to, served the community as a poet, turning theology into singable songs and readable verse, Hopkins is the opposite. His poetry was a source of great anxiety to him. He didn't know what place it should take in his spiritual life, and so it became a means of personal meditation. In terms of his contemporaries, his poetry was a failure, a mere personal diversion. Hopkins is an interesting and rare modern example of a poet not caught up in the need to publish. I think for Hopkins, poetry was secondary to things more crucial to him such as obedience to his community, his society and to his teaching – the teaching and examining that drove him to an early grave. Self-expression was not the order of the day for a Jesuit priest, and we can take that as a tragedy, as a necessary sacrifice, or as a coming alongside Christ himself. What we can't see it as, though, is a helpful example of the way the Church integrates its poets. The poems remain for us as a window into a highly imaginative soul, who in time has come to nourish the inner life of the contemporary Church.

The Poet as the Outsider

This is a warning to us: we must not imagine that poetry will ever be neatly contained. As a spiritual gift it will blow where it wills, and have its effect as much by being shunned as by being promoted. It will come from the most unlikely places. 'It will', as Hopkins put it, 'flame out like shining from shook foil.'[9] It will surprise us; I hope that, just like the poets of the First World War and the Russian poets such as Pasternak and Tsetayeva, they cannot be silenced. We must look out for the surprising voices in our own day. Unfortunately we don't find them on the bestseller shelves of W. H. Smith. Rather, we have to root them out from deep stacks and alternative bookshops, from broadsheets and brave, small publishers.

Using Hopkins as an example, I have been looking at the poet as outsider, the hermit poet, the desert poet, the poet standing over against the Church and lobbing poems into the hands of the few who can catch them. That is very much the situation of one of the finest religious poets of our time, R. S. Thomas. He has been prolifically published in his own lifetime, in receipt of the Queen's Medal for Poetry, much respected by other poets, but viewed by the Church as a perplexing phenom-enon. Rather than getting on with the poetry, they ask the questions: 'Does he believe in God? Is he a good parson? What are his sermons like? What position does he take up with regard to the institution of the Church?' What I think he has done for people of my generation in the Church is to make waiting, watching, seeing and silence acceptable means of dialogue with a difficult God. He knows the perils and pitfalls of a rural ministry, having dealt with leather-hearted farmers, the onrush of the tourist, and the selling-out to the machine. He has given us back the cross as the image of our day.

> Few possessions; a chair,
> a table, a bed
> to say my prayers by,
> and, gathered from the shore,
> the bone-like crossed sticks proving that nature
> acknowledges the Crucifixion.
> All night I am at
> a window not too small
> to be frame to the stars
> that are no further off

than the city lights
I have rejected. By day
the passers-by, who are not pilgrims, stare
    through the
rain's bars, seeing me as a prisoner
of the one view, I who
have been made free
by the tide's pendulum truth
that the heart that is low now
will be at the full tomorrow.[10]

Staying for just a little longer with 'the awkward squad' standing aslant to the Church, certainly outside its mainstream liturgy, its institutional hierarchies, and probably the taste and experience of most members of the Church, voices crying in the wilderness; staying with this area, how do we account for such a mainstream position given to the anguished cries of the psalmist?

Poetry in the Tradition

There is something about the best poetry that is above time. So when we talk about literature, and put it beside the word 'millennium', there is a danger that we will forget literature's great gift of getting to the heart of things outside the dimension of linear time. In this, religion and literature share a room; poetry, with its sharpened point of word-choice, and polished crystal of rhythm, does it very powerfully. The psalms are the most resilient of religious texts. Can we ever imagine a future without them? The psalms stand as a great overture to the theme of religion and poetry. In our own tradition, they stand about as far away as the eye can see, and yet they are so amazingly present to us.

These poems, these psalms, that seem so personal, have brought the voice of the outsider right into the heart of the liturgy: 'Out of the deep have I cried' (Psalm 130:1); 'My God, My God, why have you forsaken me?' (Psalm 22:1); 'O that I had the wings of a dove' (Psalm 55:7); 'The waters have come up, even to my neck' (Psalm 69:1); 'I am become like a vulture in the wilderness' (Psalm 102:7). It is fascinating to imagine how these personal cries from the depths made it into the lifeblood of the Hebrew liturgy. You can understand how the praise of God would be easily accepted as a staple diet of worship, but to allow the whole range of human emotion into these holy books is a remarkable achievement. They came in late, that's for sure, into what we describe as the Wisdom section. Some scholars speak of them as being not personal but community laments, suffering felt by a whole community, and therefore suitable, indeed essential, for their time spent in public dialogue with God. The psalms were also Jesus' poetrybook, material which he absorbed, prayed, lived with, died with, which reminds me of St John Chrysostom's words on the psalms:

If we keep vigil in the church, David comes first, last and midst. If early in the morning we seek for the melody of hymns, first, last and midst is David again. If we are occupied with the funeral solemnities of the departed, if virgins sit at home and spin, David is first, last and midst . . . In monasteries, amongst those holy choirs of angelic armies, David is first, midst, and last. In the convents of virgins, where are bands of them that imitate Mary; in the deserts, where are men crucified to this world and having their conversations with God, first, midst and last is he.[11]

Here are examples of individuals, poets and communities exploring the inner weather of their relationship with God, some poems remaining resolutely outside the wall, and others, such as the psalms, brought right into the Holy of Holies. This will continue, the personal God speaking to the person, drawing out from each of them their own configurations, the self-expression that has been such a healing experience for prisoners, the mentally ill, the abused, and the homeless. The telling of the story is part of the healing. These contemporary psalms will always be a necessary gloss to the psalms of David. The Psalter must speak in community and listen for the echo.

When the Abbess had admitted Caedmon into the community as a brother, she ordered him to be instructed in the events of sacred history. So Caedmon stored up in his memory all that he learned, and like one of the clean animals chewing the cud, turned it into such melodious verse that his delightful renderings turned his instructors into auditors. He sang of the creation of the world, the origin of the human race, and the whole story of Genesis. He sang of Israel's exodus from Egypt, the entry into the

Promised Land, and many other events of scriptural history. He sang of the Lord's incarnation, passion, resurrection, and ascension into Heaven, the coming of the Holy Spirit, and the teaching of the Apostles.[12]

Here with the example of Caedmon we see one of the main ways in which the poet and the Church have come together in a more public, institutional way, where poets have taken the sacred tradition and versified it. Caedmon is one example, and there are many, many more. At random and with no depth of discussion we can think of Milton taking the great theme of *Paradise Lost* and *Paradise Regained*, and in *Samson Agonistes*, instructing people in the biblical story but infusing it with all the power that comes of personal experience (in this case, blindness):

> O loss of sight, of thee I most complain!
> Blind among enemies, O worse than chains,
> Dungeon, or beggary, or decrepit age!
> Light, the prime work of God, to me is extinct,
> . . .
> Oh dark, dark, dark, amid the blaze of noon,
> Irrecoverably dark, total eclipse
> Without all hope of day.[13]

The eighth-century *Dream of the Rood* is a vivid re-enactment of the Passion of Christ as experienced by the cross itself, anthropomorphized as a soldier holding up Christ in the heat of the battle. Just a few lines give a flavour:

Men carried me
Upon their shoulders, set me on a hill,
A host of enemies there fastened me.
And then I saw the Lord of all mankind
Hasten with eager zeal that He might mount
Upon me. I dare not against God's word
Bend down or break, when I saw tremble all
The surface of the earth. Although I might
Have struck down all the foes, yet stood I fast.
Then the young hero (who was God Almighty)
Got ready, resolute and strong in heart.
He climbed onto the lofty gallows-tree,
Bold in the sight of many watching men,
When He intended to redeem mankind.[14]

We must imagine a context – perhaps a public reading in Holy Week in the monastic community at Lichfield? There were opportunities in the community to employ and to benefit from the skills of the poet.

When I have talked about this subject of religion and literature before, one of the contributions to the debate people come up with, particularly members of the Free Churches, is 'what about the hymn?' Certainly the Church has rarely been without its hymnwriters, from the earliest days. There are even gem-like hymns within the New Testament itself. The hymn has been one of the most successful ways in which the poet has communicated, in a central place in the life of the Church, in co-operation with musicians, and that must also include anthems, in which poems of a more complicated rhythm can be set and sung. I can't resist at this point recounting a story which taught me a lot about hymns, and about people who love hymns.

On a recent summer holiday in north Northumberland I got into conversation with a big dour Scotsman who lived at, or in, Flodden Field, and I presume ate Englishmen for breakfast. He asked me what I did for a living, and imagining that anything other than a prize boxer or a Border raider would have appeared unduly wimpish, I took my courage in both hands, stared at him about the chest and said, 'I'm a parson.'

'Ah,' he said, 'a Ministerr! D'ye preach a guid serrrmon?'

With customary humility I said, 'Well, it's difficult to tell.'

'You mean they don't tell you!'

'Well they don't seem . . .'

And so it went on. He was warming to the fight, and I was trying to hide under a stone. 'What else d'ye do? All ministerrs have a sideline . . .'

'Well, actually, I write poetry.'

'Hymns?'

'No, poetry.'

He made the next move. 'I'll tell you my favourite hymn.'

Some dreadful possibilities flashed through my mind – 'Christian dost thou see them'; 'Washed in the Blood of the Lamb'.

'My really favourite hymn is by Bianco da Siena.'

I gulped. This was class. All I could remember was that it was a hymn translated by Littledale, but I couldn't for the life of me remember the title.

He supplied it. ' "Come down, O Love divine". Now there's a guid hymn.'

It is amazing how committed people are to hymns, and a moving surprise when someone I had misread restores my faith in hymnody of real quality.

I shall bring in one more case study before trying to make some conclusions. How could I omit the work of George Herbert? What would he have to say for himself about the new millennium? I think he would say 'Survive the necessary struggle between God and the world, but don't lose God in the process', and secondly, 'use all the new learning, and put it to work for the Lord'.

The Poetic World of George Herbert

George Herbert must be the best-known parson-poet, the archetypal parson-poet, and he has written himself into the mind of the Church as the representative parish priest, the exemplar. The complication in the story of George Herbert is that he was a parish priest for only three years at the conclusion of his short life, although he wrote religious verse from about the age of 15. We set him up as a benchmark of clerical perfection, but I don't think he would recognize the role. He was working as a self-conscious writer, with the ability to draw on many sources, as well as his own very brief experience of the ordained life. Herbert has two main areas of expertise. The first is what we see in the poems before he was ordained, which describe the struggle he had to move out of self-concern and ambition into obedience to the will of God. That's the first area it seems to me that we take into the new millennium, the struggle.

41

I struck the board, and cry'd, No more.
                    I will abroad.
What? shall I ever sigh and pine?
My lines and life are free; free as the rode,
          Loose as the winde, as large as store.
                    Shall I be still in suit?
          Have I no harvest but a thorn
     To let me bloud, and not restore
What I have lost with cordial fruit?
                    Sure there was wine
Before my sighs did dry it: there was corn
     Before my tears did drown it.
          Is the year only lost to me?
          Have I no bays to crown it?
No flowers, no garlands hay? All blasted?
                    All wasted?
Not so, my heart: but there is fruit,
                    And thou has hands.
          Recover all thy sigh-blown age
On double pleasures: leave thy cold dispute
     Of what is fit, and not. Forsake thy cage,
                    Thy rope of sands,
Which pettie thoughts have made, and made to thee
          Good cable to enforce and draw,
                    And be thy law,
While thou didst wink and wouldst not see.
                    Away; take heed:
                    I will abroad.
Call in thy deaths head there; tie up thy fears.

> He that forebears
> To suit and serve his need,
> Deserves his load.
> But as I rav'd and grew more fierce and wilde
> At every word,
>
> Me thoughts I heard one calling, Child!
> And I reply'd, My Lord![15]

The second area of expertise is the way Herbert used the prevailing, and at the time, modish style of writing poetry, which came to be known as 'metaphysical'. It was a style of writing which did justice to the mind-heart. It had the thew of the heart and the sinew of the mind, so that the poet could think and feel at the same time. Herbert was a clever man, widely read in Renaissance literature; he was the Public Orator at Cambridge University, aware of the great upsurge in literature and drama and poetry that was going on in his time. The exciting thing is to see how he put this to work with a very simple and crystal-clear love of God and the Church.

After his poem about struggle, here is a poem of transition, 'The Elixir', where the clever use of images help Herbert to talk about the way into a deeper spirituality:

> Teach me, my God and King
> In all things thee to see,
> And what I do in anything,
> To do it as for thee:

Not rudely, as a beast,
   To runne into an action;
But still to make thee prepossest,
   And give it his perfection.

A man that looks on glasse:
   On it may stay his eye;
Or if he pleaseth, through it passe,
   And then the heav'n espie.

All may of thee partake:
   Nothing can be so mean,
Which with this tincture (for thy sake)
   Will not grow bright and clean.

A servant with this clause
   Makes drudgerie divine:
Who sweeps a room, as for thy laws,
   Makes that and th'action fine.

This is the famous stone
   That turneth all to gold:
For that which God doth touch and own
   Cannot for lesse be told.[16]

Glass, tinctures, touchstones, servants: we are far from
the world of ploughs and sheep. It is a world closer to
the stately rooms of Wilton House, not a stone's throw
from Herbert's church at Fugglestone. We see in this
poem renaissance man, in the process of tincturing and
turning the material of his cultured, intellectual and

social world into something gold in the eyes of God, a life of service in the ordained ministry. It is the breadth of the range of religious emotion that interests me about George Herbert, and the enjoyment he had in getting his poems to work in just the way he wanted. He was a consummate artist, with that mysticism of the everyday, which has so characterized the English religious temperament.

Herbert was never really very well. The Cambridge weather cannot have helped, and however much the joys of being married to Jane, and settling into a parish near Wilton House meant to him, after three years, at the age of 33, he was dead (not before, however, he wrote those poems which he never expected to be published, except that his friend Nicholas Ferrar thought it would help some poor souls). Many people are familiar with the poem 'Love', the third of the poems by that name and placed as the final poem of his collection.

Love bade me welcome: yet my soul drew back
    Guiltie of dust and sinne.
But quick-eyed love, observing me grow slack
    From my first entrance in,
Drew nearer to me, sweetly questioning,
    If I lack'd anything.

A guest I answer'd, worthy to be here:
    Love said, You shall be he.
I the unkind, ungrateful? Ah my deare,
    I cannot look on thee.

Love took my hand, and smiling did reply,
    Who made the eyes but I?

Truth Lord, but I have marr'd them: let my shame
    Go where it doth deserve
And know you not, says Love, who bore the blame?
    My deare, then I will serve.
You must sit down, sayes Love, and taste my meat:
    So I did sit and eat.[17]

And What of the Future?

I end with some radical, millennial conclusions, which lie for me in the area of poets' need for some sort of community within which to work. Moving to Winchester from Cumberland, I moved into a depth of Church tradition which I am only just beginning to tap. There was in Winchester a great flowering of the arts from the time of Alfred in 850 until about 1100, with the turn of the first millennium as its peak. Alfred himself wrote poetry. Two poems he attached as a Preface to the translation into Anglo-Saxon of St Gregory the Great's *Liber Regulae Pastoralis* (known as the *Pastoral Care*), believed to have been written in 591. This poem uses the image of the water that flows so profusely through Winchester over its chalk bed, and Alfred writes that he hopes the Holy Spirit will similarly flow through the Church and the lives of its saints:

These are waterscapes that God had promised
as a comfort to the world,

He said that he would wish for evermore
that living waters should flow into the world,
from the hearts of all beneath the sky,
that faithfully believe in him. There is little doubt
these waterscapes their wellspring have
in heaven, that is the Holy Ghost,
from which the saints and chosen ones can draw.[18]

Alfred was eager that the works of Christian literature should be available to those who only understood Anglo-Saxon. He invited Grimbald, and other monk-scholars from France, to come to help him. At the same time he encouraged the setting up of monastic communities. His wife Aelswith founded a Benedictine convent in Winchester. I have been involved recently in translating the passion prayers of an eighth-century manuscript, the Book of Nunnaminster, which shows the important place of women in the intellectual life of the Anglo-Saxon Church. The crucial place of the committed community under the Rule of St Benedict was the ideal setting for an Anglo-Saxon renaissance of the Word. Liturgy was given a central place and its reform is recorded in the 'Regularis Concordia'. Aelfric (955–1020), wrote the first grammar book to help the young monks versed in Anglo-Saxon to learn Latin, and all this alongside a great flourishing of other arts – calligraphy, illumination of manuscripts, needlework – all centred on the word of Scripture, which in turn is centred on God in Trinity.

The Church of England of today is in an interesting position. It is numerically small but its residual influence is wide. Am I being foolish if I hope for some sort of resurgence of Christian community, which is unlikely to be monastic as it was in Alfred's day, but a Christian community in which the poet takes his or her place among the other necessary talents which move a Christian community on its rightful way? Pure poets were shunned from early monastic communities, and knowing a few, I can see why. When it comes to the Christian faith, poetry is not the main thing. A heady concern merely for words has never been the hallmark of a disciple of Christ. The central thing is Christ himself, and the worship of God in Trinity. Poetry, the making and shaping of words and meanings, and sentences that move the heart and mind and soul through use of image, rhythms, sound and colour in language is a tool, but that tool has to be kept sharpened, and the poets in the Christian community need various things to help them do their work, and in the Church today these resources are not as much valued as they should be. Poets, unfortunately, are usually the last people to be able to get their act together to do anything about it.

When the poet Mayakovsky was writing poetry in Russia just after the Revolution, he gave some wonderful groundrules for what a poet needed to be of service, in his case to the State. It transposes well to the needs of a poet writing for the Church. 'What, then, are the necessary conditions for getting one's poetic work started?' His answer was this:

1. The existence of a social task that can be accomplished only through poetic work. There must be

a social command. *[I would add there must be a gospel or religious command.]*

2. You must have an exact knowledge of or at least a feeling for aspirations of the class or group you represent. *[I would add you need to have at least a feeling for the aspirations of the community you live in.]*

3. You must have the material, the words. The store-houses, the reserves of your mind should be equipped with the necessary words – expressive, rare, new, renovated, and invented words of every kind. *[I couldn't agree more.]*

4. Means of production are necessary. These include a pen, a pencil, a typewriter, a telephone, a pipe or cigarettes, clothes to wear when going out for food, a bicycle to ride on to the editorial office, a table, an umbrella to enable one to write in the rain, a room in which one can take a certain number of steps (this is necessary for one's work), connections with a news-clipping bureau in order to make sure of receiving a continual supply of material on subjects that are of interest to your district.

5. One must have formed the habit of elaborating words. This habit is infinitely individual, and comes only after years of daily work. It covers rhymes, metres, alliterations, images, gradations, styles, pathos, titles, plans, and so on.[19]

I would add to that, time to be still and let the poems make their journey from out there, into your mind and heart, and through to your hand; a good, no, a brilliant, no, the *best* library in Western Christendom to let you feed on the tradition; colleagues who understand and use you for what you can do and not for what you can't; the opportunity to keep in touch with poets of all cultures, religions and nationalities.

I really think that the Church needs a new renaissance. We have too long neglected words, and the sister of words, silence. We have been too busy, too dependent on keeping up with the machine, human and mechanical, and getting everything right administratively. We need people working together from their strengths. Our theologians need to draw from the world of the poets, that is, they should attend to the *logos* and the *logoi*, the Word and the words. How people imagine the Word can survive if the words are not in some way up to conveying the Word is beyond me. Better silence than pap.

I don't feel very comfortable in the world of the prophet's musts; I have for too long been a hermit poet. Do cathedrals need poets in residence, or does the Province of Canterbury need a Poet Laureate? All power to Andrew Motion's new laureateship if he can encourage poetry in schools, and create space, time and finance for writers to write. For myself, I'm much happier in my own community trying to write the words both that it wants, and that it needs, in order to point out to people the riches of the poetic tradition, to write prayers when needed, and to advise on the rhythm of the psalms in new translation. Such creative and enjoyable tasks might, just might, bring white hairs to a quiet grave. They had an enchanting influence on the end of Caedmon's life.

'Dear sons, my heart is at peace with all the servants of God.' Then, when he had fortified himself with the heavenly Viaticum, he prepared to enter the other life, and asked how long it would be before the brothers were roused to sing God's praises in the Night Office. 'Not long,' they replied.

'Good, then let us wait till then,' he answered; and signing himself with the Holy Cross, he laid his head on the pillow and passed away quietly in his sleep.[20]

Notes

1. Bede, *Ecclesiastical History of the English People* (trans. Leo Sherley-Price; Harmondsworth: Penguin Books, 1955), p. 248 (author's own translation).
2. Dylan Thomas, 'A Winter's Tale', in his *Collected Poems* (London: J. M. Dent, 1952), p. 122.
3. Quoted in René Hayne, *David Jones* (Cardiff: University of Wales Press, 1975), pp. 57, 58.
4. C. C. Abbott (ed.), *The Correspondence of Gerard Manley Hopkins and Richard Watson Dixon* (Oxford University Press, 1970), p. 14 (5 October 1878).
5. N. H. Mackenzie (ed.), *The Poetical Works of Gerard Manley Hopkins* (Oxford: Clarendon Press, 1999).
6. Mackenzie, *ibid.*, p. 181.
7. Mackenzie, *ibid.*, p. 181.
8. Mackenzie, *ibid.*, p. 182.
9. Mackenzie, *ibid.*, p. 139.
10. R. S. Thomas, 'At the End', in his *No Truce with the Furies* (Newcastle: Bloodaxe Books, 1995), p. 42.
11. Quoted in C. A. Briggs, *Psalms* 5, Volume 1 (Edinburgh: T. & T. Clark, 1906), p. xciv.
12. Bede, *Ecclesiastical History*, p. 249.

13. John Milton, 'Samson Agonistes', lines 69–72 and 82–84.
14. *Dream of the Rood*, in Richard Hamer (ed.), *A Choice of Anglo-Saxon Verse* (London: Faber & Faber, 1970), p. 163.
15. 'The Collar' from F. E. Hutchinson (ed.), *The Works of George Herbert* (Oxford: Clarendon Press, 1941), pp. 153–4.
16. Hutchinson, *ibid.*, pp. 184–5.
17. Hutchinson, *ibid.*, pp. 188–9.
18. 'The Metrical Epilogue to the Pastoral Care'. Author's own translation.
19. H. Marshall, *Mayakovsky and His Poetry* (Bombay: Current Book House, 1955), pp. 192–3.
20. Bede, *Ecclesiastical History*, p. 250.

Christianity and Modernity

A. N. WILSON

Christianity Demythologized

The millennium is the anniversary of an event in which we no longer believe: namely, the birth of Almighty God in human form in a stable in Bethlehem. You might think that there was nothing very odd about human scepticism on this point. After all, it does stretch credulity to believe that a virgin could conceive. How, at this date in history, knowing all that we know about human biology, could we possibly claim that Christianity was literally true? But unbelief in the story of Bethlehem – and with it, unbelief in Christianity itself – is different in kind from unbelief in, say, Judaism or Islam or Buddhism. For those who were in the vanguard of destroying the Christian faith over the last 200 years were not a tiny handful of atheist philosophers and agnostic scientists. It was the Christians themselves. That is what is unique about the collapse of Christianity, as opposed to the decline or crisis in other world religions – if, indeed, such a decline or crisis is happening. Christianity will decline yet further in the next thousand years – decline, I would predict to the point of near extinction – because Christians themselves no longer believe it to be true.

Already, I can hear the tops being taken off biros, and nibs being dipped in green ink, as fervent believers in Christian doctrine write to the publishers asking how such an unbelieving rascal as myself could be trusted to discuss so sacred a theme. It may interest Mr Wilson to know that the authors of these as-yet unwritten letters believe in every jot and tittle of Christian teaching! They believe in the Virgin Birth, and the Resurrection of Jesus, and his bodily Ascension into Heaven. They believe that Jesus thought it was his mission, while on earth, to found a new religion, quite distinct from his own religion of Judaism. To prove that this was his intention, he instituted a new Sacrament – the Lord's Supper, or the Eucharist or the Mass. Before being gathered into the clouds, he told his 12 disciples, the forebears of the bishops and priests of today, that they should go and teach all nations this new doctrine, and baptize them in the name of the Father, the Son and the Holy Ghost. How, pray, can Mr Wilson say that these things are not true? Let me make myself clear. I am not bringing myself into this discussion at all. I am not saying that 2000 years of Christian history are null and void because one small individual, writing at the beginning of the new millennium, cannot put his hand on his heart and say that he believes another human being walked on water or changed water into wine.

I am saying that if you went to a theological seminary, or a university where religion was being taught; if you went to a college where they were training ministers of

the gospel; if you studied the Bible using the most searching and honest commentaries, written by men and
women who had devoted a lifetime of scholarship to
the subject, you would find only a minority of these
scholars professing old-fashioned, fully orthodox Christian belief. Oh, you would find that many of them were
priests or ministers of their particular church. You
would find that they attended the various rites of those
churches. But ask them, 'Do you believe that God
Almighty took human flesh in the person of Jesus?' and
I suspect you would find only a minority able to say an
unambiguous 'Yes!' Do they believe that Jesus was born
in Bethlehem? Only a tiny handful of Bible scholars
believe that. Fewer, I should guess, believe that he was
born of a virgin. Many would say that they believed in
the Resurrection, but ask them to say in detail whether
they believed in the Gospel accounts of an empty tomb,
and you will find that they do not. This is not the place
to enter in detail into why this great cloud of witnesses,
stretching back over 150 years, no longer believe in
Christianity in the formal, old-fashioned sense. I am
just observing an empirical fact: most theologians and
Christian scholars do not believe in what most laymen
and laywomen think of as Christianity.

A small example. Many scholars – not all – consider
it impossible that Jesus, a pious Jew, could ever have
instituted the Eucharist in which he is supposed to have
given a cup of wine to his followers and said, 'This is
my blood'. Even if he spoke symbolically; even if you
do not accept, as Roman Catholics used to do, that the
cup contained real blood, you would still have to think

55

of a pious Jew deliberately breaking one of the deepest
Jewish taboos – the taboo against drinking blood. A
pious Catholic, however, might say in reply, 'Haven't
you read the Gospel?' In John's Gospel, Jesus says,
'Those who eat my flesh and drink my blood have eternal life' (6:56). This is where scholars and 'ordinary'
people divide. There might be scholars who in some
sense 'believe' in the Eucharist. Certainly there are plenty
of scholars who still go to Mass. But you would find it
difficult to find any scholar who thought that the Fourth
Gospel contained the actual verbatim words of Jesus.
What that book does is to preach late first-century Christian teaching by putting it into the mouth of the historical Jesus. It is what one scholar called a theological
novel, written decades after the real Jesus had died.
Whereas Christians in the old days – pre-nineteenth century – might have argued that John's Gospel was a work
of history, you would find no Christian scholar (outside
a tiny band of evangelical die-hards) arguing like that
today.

Christianity and Modernity

You would, of course, find plenty of rabbis who interpreted the Jewish Scriptures in more or less the same
way that rabbis were reading the Bible in the lifetime
of Jesus. You would find many – indeed nearly all –
Muslim scholars and imams reading the Holy Koran in
exactly the same sense that it was written down in the
seventh century. That is because you can still have interesting plausible arguments about God and morality,

whereas so much of Christian myth is falsifiable. It makes truth-claims that aren't true. Christianity came to a crisis point 150 years ago when all these skeletons came out of its cupboard. German biblical scholars were taking the Bible to bits at just the moment when the scientists were casting doubt on the very idea of a Creator. Now, of course, you can still go on believing that there is a God when you have read Darwin's *The Origin of Species*. The huge majority of Victorian scientists did so, and a high proportion of modern scientists believe in God or something very like him. Darwin's discoveries did, however, for many earnest seekers after truth, remove any need for positing such metaphors as purpose in nature or a mind behind the universe. Darwin revealed a process which was, so to say, self-sufficient, which did not need a *deus ex machina*. Or indeed a deus, a god, of any kind. Darwin, in fact, made more of an impact on philosophers who had already been reaching godless conclusions about life, than he did on biologists. In the 1840s and 1850s, when these great matters were being aired on a wide scale for the first time in history, the day-to-day existence of the majority in the West was abjectly wretched. It was only in 1842 that the Mines Act forbade the employment of girls and boys under the age of 10 down the mines. The sheer grind of life, the difficulty of earning enough to eat and of finding enough space to stretch out and sleep at night, dominated the existence of nearly all the inhabitants of Europe in these years when the Germans were undermining the Bible and Darwin was depicting nature itself as a universal struggle against pitiless, mindless odds. Little Jo the Crossing Sweeper in Dickens's *Bleak House* – he did not even know the Our Father – is not an invention. This was what the working classes were like in industrial Europe. Marx and Engels had every reason for believing in 1848 that religion was finished. The churchmen who dared go into the slums agreed with them: 'Religion is nowhere' in the cities, said the first Anglican bishop of Stepney.[1]

One hundred and fifty years later, the West faces a different world; a world overwhelmed, in Northern Europe and America, not so much by mindless, grinding poverty as by mindless, grinding prosperity. The Victorian poor were thin as whippets. The late twentieth-century poor are obese, stuffed with chips and sedatives to stop them rebelling against the pointless hell of existence. They know no more than their forebears of the Christian tradition; but now – this is the new thing – nor do the so-called educated classes! The Victorian middle classes wrestled with doubts because they had read in their periodicals that Sir Charles Lyell had dated the planet – by means of fossil evidence – and seen that the process of Creation took much longer than the six days of Genesis. The late twentieth-century middle classes don't know what Genesis is. They are cut off from any tradition of reading the Bible. Place the average well-educated middle class Westerner in front of a picture of a woman in blue talking to an angel. It would seem as baffling, alien and incomprehensible as a scene from Greek mythology. They wouldn't know the story to which it referred. Our Christian heritage is no longer in our bloodstream. We have lived to see a whole generation of people who were brought up not as atheists – that would suggest an interest in religion – but entirely without religion. To such a generation, the truth-claims of Christianity would sound bizarre, as would its particular moral teachings, especially those about sex.

In countries which have traditionally been bastions of conservative Catholic belief, such as Portugal or Ireland, Catholics in this generation have left the Church in droves. Few are willing to commit themselves to a life of celibate priesthood or to accept that monogamous heterosexual union for life is the only acceptable sexual option for all men and women. The numerological decline of practising Christians in the world would appear to be irreversible. The present Pope, who has done so much to defend Catholicism against the assaults of secularism, has said that if the faith continues to decline, numerically, at the present rate then in 70 years' time there will be no Christians on the face of the planet. That prophecy is perhaps pessimistic. It ignores the human capacity to be inconsistent. The Catholic bishops who have mistresses or the American millionaire evangelicals who ignore Jesus' instruction to sell all they have and give to the poor are not so much scandals as the gospel's last hope. Perhaps in America, Christianity will survive in a more or less undiluted form. A civilization that readily believes in flying saucers and the resurrection of Elvis Presley should have no difficulty in continuing to swallow what is dished out by the tele-evangelists.

A. N. Wilson

Meaning behind the Universe

Yet for most people the religious questions, when they occur to the mind, are of a deeper seriousness than this. Many human beings would still wish to echo the first great modern metaphysician, Immanuel Kant, when he said, 'Two things fill the mind with ever new and increasing admiration and awe, the more often and steadily we reflect upon them: the starry heavens above me, and the moral law within me.'[2] When all the mythologies of religion have been discarded and when all the false theories of Christianity have been exposed by patient and honest scholars, men and women of a reflective turn of mind will still remain convinced that there is underlying the universe a deep moral purpose. Lose this sense of seriousness and life becomes ultimately unendurable. Most of us are far too busy to follow the intricacies of Kant's philosophical journeyings, but we believe these things in our gut. There is a religion that satisfies this deep human need for a moral code without a mythology. It is not Christianity. As the third millennium of Christ's supposed Incarnation begins, fewer and fewer practising Christians really believe that God is Three and God is One.

What would be the point of trying to persuade themselves or others of the truth of statements which are quite meaningless? They go to church to continue to express their membership of particular communities of faith, not because they really believe as their ancestors believed. Even the Pope has told us lately that the stories of heaven and hell were just picture-language. Of course, but it would have been a help if the popes of history had said that before exploiting the lives of millions of hapless, simple people with their threats of hell and their blackmailing hint that unbaptized babies were forever in limbo separated from their mothers. In a different, vigorous tradition, there is no need to trim and change the tradition in this manner. The mullahs and the imams of Islam preach the same undiluted message which was first given to the world by the Holy Prophet in the sixth and seventh centuries. While the West tries to dub the followers of Islam fundamentalist lunatics, increasing numbers of men and women turn to the Koran and find in this book what a sizeable proportion of the human race has always craved: a moral and an intellectual acknowledgement of the lordship of God without the incumbrance of Christian mythological baggage in which almost no one really believes. That is why Christianity will decline in this millennium, and the religious hunger of the human heart will be answered by the Crescent, not by the Cross. Whether Islam accepts or rejects it, the modern doctrine of feminism will, I suspect, be the big question for religion in this millennium. But where does this leave the great imaginative tradition of Christianity which we find enshrined in our literature?

Christianity and Literature

A remarkable fact about the history of English Christianity, and in particular of Anglicanism in the middle part of the twentieth century, was the large number of poets and novelists who were not merely *pratiquantes* or *pratiquants* but who explored the faith and its implications in their writings. Think of Dorothy L. Sayers, Charles Williams, the C. S. Lewis of the science fiction trilogy and the Narnia stories (not Lewis the tub-thumping apologist of *Mere Christianity*), or the novels of Barbara Pym – all in their different ways written explorations of Church or religious life on an imaginative scale which would have surprised the agnostic generation of their parents. One remembers Ivy Compton Burnett's impatience with her contemporary Rose Macaulay when she read her final novel, *The Towers of Trebizond*, and realized that Rose had returned to the faith. 'Why can't she remain a perfectly sensible agnostic like everyone else?' Two writers stand out to my mind in this period who were most defiant in their refusal to be perfectly sensible agnostics: the first is T. S. Eliot, and the second is his sometime pupil, John Betjeman.

> If I think, again, of this place,
> and of people, not wholly commendable,
>   Of no immediate kin or kindness,
>   But some particular genius,
>   All touched by a common genius,
> United in the strife which divided them;
>   If I think of a king at nightfall,
> of three men, and more, on the scaffold
>   And a few who died forgotten
>   In other places, here and abroad,
>   and of one who died blind and quiet,
> Why should we celebrate these dead men
>   more than the dying?[3]

This is one of those resonant passages of *The Four Quartets* which must have thrilled the generation of Christians who first read it, as much as it dismayed those who felt that literature should move on, leaving this old baggage behind us. There would be many now, I suspect, to whom the lines were incomprehensible. Perhaps – dare one say – most readers of the English language would find the lines incomprehensible?

'We cannot restore old policies/Or follow an antique drum'[4] becomes a prophecy which applies very directly to the inner life of Eliot's own church. A church which seemed so alive when John Betjeman was worshipping in it only a few years ago, it would seem.

> Great red church of my parents, cruciform crossing
>   they knew –
> Over these same encaustics they and their parents
>   trod
> Bound through a red-brick transept for a once
>   familiar pew
> Where the organ set them singing and the sermon
>   let them nod
> And up this coloured brickwork the same long
>   shadows grew
> As these in the stencilled chancel where I kneel in
>   the presence of God.[5]

There can be nothing less ambiguous than this. Few poets since Herbert were more naturally at ease in church.

Wonder beyond Time's wonders, that Bread so
    white and small
Veiled in golden curtains, too mighty for men to
    see,
Is the Power which sends the shadows up this
    polychrome wall,
Is God who created the planet, the chain-smoking
    millions and me;
Beyond the throb of the engines is the throbbing
    heart of all –
Christ, at this Highbury altar, I offer myself to
    Thee.[6]

It is impossible not to be moved by this poem. Equally
it is difficult to imagine anyone writing it nowadays,
and yet it was only published some 50 years ago. I am
not saying that the imaginative possibilities of the faith
have altogether dried up. This would be impossible to
say while Geoffrey Hill was writing, and the denser, the
more difficult the poetry becomes from that pen, the
closer he seems to the heart of Christian faith. But Hill
is a good case in point. His angry poetry is precisely
concerned, it would seem for much of the time, with the
impossibility of the old words and symbols resonating in
new ears. Those of us who read the poetry of Milton
without having had a grounding in classical literature
are forever fumbling about in footnotes trying to find
out where the fountain of Arethusa was, or who the
Muse herself was whom Orpheus bore. We're hardly
reading, we are engaged in minor archaeology. No
echoes occur. Eliot was trying to bring back, by means of

pastiche architecture, the echoes of Dante, Shakespeare, Sanskrit and Mother Julian of Norwich into our common language so that we could speak with shared images and symbols. Without shared images and symbols, religion does not function. Nor does literature. Future generations will be deaf to both. Of course there are still people slipping into churches, as John Betjeman did in that moving poem, and offering themselves to Christ. (The church in question has been made redundant now – it's an Arts Centre, whatever that is.) One suspects that the number of practising Christians will fall and fall and fall throughout the coming generations to the point where mainstream Christianity becomes as esoteric as the faith of the Shakers. But even if it doesn't, the churches themselves, for reasons which are wholly opaque to the great majority of cultivated people in Europe and America, created the greatest single obstacle to the preservation of a Christian tradition in the future.

The Rise of Liturgical Revisionism

Sine the nineteenth century there have been strides forward in each generation in the field of biblical scholarship, and that is something in which we can all rejoice. Inevitably it would lead to fresh translations of the Bible as new understandings emerged. But did this really necessitate the abolition of the time-honoured seventeenth-century translation in its liturgical context? The Church of Rome had been tinkering with its liturgy throughout the twentieth century, altering the Easter

ceremonies in ways which would be barely noticeable
to those who were not obsessives. But what can have
possessed them to abolish the so-called Tridentine mass,
a liturgy which was in essence 1000 years older than
the Council of Trent? Eager to show that it could be as
modern as Rome, the Church of England, which had a
perfectly good vernacular liturgy, and which had
developed since 1928 a perfectly workable way of add-
ing local variations to it if and when required, chose to
concoct what is quite possibly the most disgracefully
ugly and unmemorable liturgy ever devised in the history
of the human race. I won't be a bore and go through
either the *Alternative Service Book* or the *Missa
Normativa* and give examples of the many infelicities
which it has introduced. By abolishing the vocative, it
makes all its addresses to the Godhead seem like police
statements read back to an unfortunate victim in the
dock. 'From age to age you gathered a people to
yourself . . .' How inelegant, and how meaningless to
have changed the immemorial liturgical exchange '*Dom-
inus vobiscum. Et cum spiritu tuo*' into '*The Lord be
with you. And also with you.*' It recalls the exchanges
of schoolchildren: 'the same to you with brass knobs
on'.

Why did they do it? What utter lunacy, what blas-
phemous arrogance, possessed them? Why did they
think that their decades – the 1960s and 1970s – were
so superior to anything which had gone before that they
could uproot, change and uglify time-honoured liturgical routines which had sustained the generation of
Queen Elizabeth, of Launcelot Andrews and the Royal

Martyr, of Pepys and Dryden and Queen Anne; of Dean
Swift and Samuel Johnson; of Coleridge and Words-
worth and Sir Walter Scott (who was converted from
Presbyterianism by the liturgy and the liturgy alone); of
the Victorian doubters, and by those – Eliot and Betjeman and Rose Macaulay included – who in the twentieth
century, returned, awe-struck and blinking with amaze-
ment, to the altar of God and to faith? In each and every
case what they returned to was the faith which was
embodied in certain words, words which had always
been adapted, modified and altered from place to place
in small ways, but which remained fundamentally the
same. There is a very moving moment in the life of the
great French modernist the Abbé Hébert who imagined
himself at a High Mass in the Duomo at Pisa – hard by
the very place, incidentally, where John Ruskin had a
highly comparable epiphany.

I listened, and I heard these words –

> Sub diversis speciebus,
> Signis tantum et non rebus,
> Latent res eximiae!

I started. It was a complete expression of my own
thoughts. Appearances, signs, symbols, which veil the
mysterious reality, but which nevertheless adapt us to
it, so that it penetrates us and makes us live – is not
this one of the essential elements of all faith and of
all philosophy?[7]

A. N. Wilson

Hébert imagines himself hearing the old eucharistic theology of Aquinas, and interpreting it in a purely modern way. Another modernist was to describe God himself as 'la dernière idole'.

The Roman Catholic Church's reaction to the modernist movement was an imaginative disaster. Pius X simply failed to see that for most men and women of faith in the twentieth century it was not a possibility to pretend to adopt the thought processes of an earlier age. By insisting, for example, that every Catholic could prove the existence of God to his or her own satisfaction he must have driven literally millions from the practice of the faith. Of course, the millions who stay feel comfortable behind the stockade. But the cause of truth has not been advanced very helpfully by such conservative gesturings. The modernists called for the old symbols and the old words to be interpreted in ways which made sense to modern people. And in many cases, of course, that meant not interpreting them at all. Most of us who have felt that any time we have spent in church was unwasted recall either moments of silence, or moments when music was playing. But utterly to change the words and the furniture! This removes the possibility of our all partaking in the one shared symbol. It introduces new and facile expressions which grate on the ear, and incidentally destroys one of the principal functions of liturgical recitations whether of the Scriptures or of the sacramental mystery – namely, that one generation passes on to the next the words and experiences of its predecessors.

We are born with the dead:
See, they return, and bring us with them.
The moment of the rose and the moment of the
    yew-tree
Are of equal duration. A people without history
Is not redeemed from time, for history is a pattern
Of timeless moments . . .[8]

The liturgy was above all a pattern of timeless moments, daily repeated in quires and places where they sing. It was a far more important function of the Church than 'Thought for the Day', or the woefully misdirected and ill-judged attempts to speak in the language of young people, or to teach imagined categories of being far beyond the ken of the average parson – such mythical beings as ordinary people, or people in inner cities. The liturgy was for all sorts and conditions of people. Its very impersonality, its lack of chumminess, its failure to attempt relevance, was what made it timelessly and irreplaceably relevant.

There is no point in Latin Mass Societies or Prayer Book Societies. Much as we sympathize with the die-hards and the nostalgic brigade, they are crying to the moon. The damage was done when Common Prayer ceased to be Common Prayer and when in the great Western Church, a unifying language, far more unifying than Esperanto, a truly universal tongue in which the human race could voice its deepest prayers and yearnings in a debased version of the language of the Caesars, was replaced by the Babel-sound of multilingual masses. At least no other language known to me has attempted the ugliness of 'and also with you' – all the other European tongues keep the mysterious liturgical politesse of '*et cum spiritu tuo*'. I'm inclined to think that really it is as simple as that. The Church abolished itself. No one asked it to do this, and most of its members were horrified when it did so. No converts came in because of Series III or the *Missa Normativa*, they came in either in spite of these things or as a result of religious experiences denied to the rest of us but which in any generation will occur, to comfort some and to baffle others.

The Responsibility of the Clergy

I am not talking about those few – few when compared with the huge numbers with no experience of the Christian faith at all – who have had a direct experience of God or of Jesus. I am talking about how faith might be communicated to a future age, or how it might be understood imaginatively by writers, above all perhaps by poets. And I don't see how it can be now, because its common language has been vandalized and destroyed by the clergy. I have to say that we hate the clergy quite a lot for this, and it is one of the reasons that many of us, who used to love the Church, and who still love the old buildings and the ancient music, find that our affection for the institutional Church has all but evaporated. I am talking about that Barbara Pym-ish love of all things churchy – it is hard to imagine many imaginative people sustaining it in the future. Her own diaries reflect the distress and disappointment felt by a pious woman in central London in search of unwrecked liturgy in her lunch-hours. There was something so arrogant about the changes. It implied that we could throw away what had been for others the means of grace, the symbols of the ultimate mystery, and make up our own version. Typical of the ethos of the thing is the habit which came in, almost as soon as the liturgy changed, of little spontaneous homilies being spoken after the Gospel even at Low Mass – as though the busy office worker or shopper in the middle of Norwich or Rome or Paris would want to hear five minutes of banal thoughts made up on the spur of the moment – rather than the old words, the tried and trusted words, the words which, worn and smooth like old, well-trodden stones, had been heard so often before, and which had so often been found to nourish and to sustain, regardless of the doubts and dryness and emptiness of those who heard them.

If Christianity had suffered the intellectual blows of the last two centuries; if it had provided the unsatisfactory answers which it did do to the questions of the Darwinians, or to those who worried about what sense, if at all, one could any longer believe in the Bible; if Christianity had given, I say, anything other than a feeble response intellectually to all these difficulties, it might yet have survived. But I cannot see how it can survive in anything like the form which previous generations of Christians, for the last 1950 years, would have recognized as Christian, now that it has departed from the concept of an orally transmitted faith. But this is all commonplace. No intelligent person outside the ranks of the clergy and the professional churchgoers, the Synod

71

busybodies and committee members questions any of it for a moment. Just read Stevie Smith's two poems 'Why are the Clergy . . . ?' and 'How do you see?'. They say all that I have been trying to say.

> Why are the clergy of the Church of England
> Always altering the words of the prayers in the
>   Prayer Book?[9]

> Oh Christianity, Christianity,
> Why do you not answer our difficulties?[10]

The modernist crisis was a tragedy not just for the Roman Catholics whom it directly affected but for the human race. And in differing ways we have been repeating it ever since. None of the lessons of Pius X's disastrous mistakes has been learned. We still find those honest seekers after truth who do not wish to discard all our spiritual baggage from the past, but equally who do not wish to dress in the pretend clothes of yesterday's thoughts vilified as heretics. There is talk of introducing heresy trials in the Church of England for those who will not say they believe that the virginal conception of Christ was a historical event in the same verifiable historic sense that the relief of Mafeking was true. The leadership of the churches is dishonest. There is no other word for it – unless you add cowardly. They have been theologically educated. They know that these concepts – such as the physical Resurrection or the Virgin Birth – are not 'true' as history; indeed, they know that to believe in their historical truth is to begin on a trail of

– such as the physical Resurrection or the Virgin Birth – are not 'true' as history; indeed, they know that to believe in their historical truth is to begin on a trail of mistakes which will inevitably end in what was once called bad theology. But they do not dare, even at the beginning of this new millennium, to rock the boat. As a result, nearly all of us stay outside the Church and watch its gradual decline with a mixture of sorrow and *Schadenfreude*. What else does an organization expect, which so consistently refuses to be intellectually serious?

We come to church to be serious and we expect serious responses to the doubts and philosophical changes which have happened to all of us, Jew and Gentile, bond and free, in the last 200 years. We do not expect kindergarten squabbles about miracles. Christianity for all serious purposes invented a way of looking at human nature and the inner life which is part and parcel of our very civilization. It invented the inner life – well, St Augustine in many ways invented the inner life. There is no need to believe in consciousness – many psychologists from William James onwards would say there was no such thing. There is no need to believe in individualism – the physicalist school of psychology/philosophy would discourage any such faith. Yet many of us feel that not to nourish these myths – notions of soul, individualism, personhood – is to erode an important part of our self-consciousness not only as individuals but also as a society. Islam, the only viable religion of the future, has other excellent things to give the human race – these have included mathematics, and many good jokes. But there is no tradition of great Islamic novels. That is why Rushdie is a boring novelist and Proust so eternally fascinating. The novel – the great expression of the idea that here are different persons, millions of them, flitting about the planet being different from one another – derives directly from the Christian fiction of a soul.

> For who would lose,
> Though full of pain . . .
> Those thoughts that wander through eternity . . .[11]

This a deeply humanistic, deeply Christian concept, deriving in part, of course, from the Jewish conception of the inner life in the Psalms, but very much as filtered through and reinterpreted by the Western Church fathers. Many of our art forms in the past are based on it, but so too are some of our political institutions such as the notion of a democracy in which everyone's voice counts. The Christian tradition is the place from whence springs much of what we cherish. Christian artists are often those who have managed a synthesis of ideas which appear to destroy the old but actually invigorate it: think of Dante, who almost single-handedly made Aquinas imaginatively accessible. Aquinas was the genius who managed to make the discoveries of Arab mathematics and logic, the writings of Averroes, the rediscovery of Aristotle – none of them notably compatible with the orthodoxies of Christianity – into a new synthesis by which the human race could understand itself, talk to itself about itself, for another 400 years. What happened in the nineteenth century was that no Aquinas arose, and no Dante to absorb Darwinism, Determinism, Freudianism or

Marxian materialism, or 'perfectly sensible agnosticism'.
The modernists tried to invent such a synthesis, but how
could they urge intelligent and broadminded people to
join a Church which was persecuting them? The same
pattern, alas, repeats itself throughout our times, and
now that the habit of learning the old Christian stories
and prayers has all but died out, and now that Christianity has, as they say, turned itself back into a sect, there
really seems to be no future. There will be Christians in
the next generation, but we can be sadly certain that
there will be no Christian literature – that came to an
end with the generation of T. S. Eliot.

Notes

1. George Forres Brown, *Reflections of a Bishop 1915*.
2. Immanuel Kant, *Critique of Pure Reason* (1788), p. 2.
3. T. S. Eliot, 'Little Gidding III', *The Four Quartets* in *The Complete Poems and Plays of T. S. Eliot*, (London: Faber, 1969),
   pp. 195–6.
4. Eliot, 'Little Gidding III', p. 196.
5. John Betjeman, 'St Saviour's. Aberdeen Park, Highbury,
   London', in his *Collected Poems* (London: John Murray, 1958),
   p. 155.
6. Betjeman, 'St Saviour's', pp. 155–6.
7. Marcel Hébert, quoted in A. R. Vidler, *A Variety of Catholic
   Modernists* (Cambridge: Cambridge University Press, 1970),
   p. 67.
8. Eliot, 'Little Gidding V', in *The Four Quartets*, p. 197.
9. Stevie Smith, 'Why are the Clergy . . . ?', in her *Collected Poems*
   (London: Allen Lane, 1975), p. 335.
10. Stevie Smith, 'How do You See', in *Collected Poems*, p. 416.
11. John Milton, *Paradise Lost*, Book 2, 1.146.

Religion and the Rise of Fiction

PENELOPE LIVELY

Literature and the Millennium

This series of reflections addresses the subject of religion, literature and the future, poised as we are at the beginning of a new millennium – and that word immediately gives pause for thought, thought that is entirely relevant to an argument I want to put forward about the writing of fiction. The concept of a millennium is itself an attempt to corral time, to impose a structure where structure there is none. Beyond the structures of nature – the turning of the world, the lunar calendar – time refuses to be orderly. It simply streams away, ahead of us and behind, without beginning or end. And the human mind finds this hard to contemplate – or at least the mind of anyone who is not a physicist does. Christianity decided that time should be pinned firmly to the central event of Christian mythology, thus ensuring that the birth of Christ would be remembered with an outburst of some of the most extravagant secular junketings the world had ever seen.

The approach of the first millennium had a rather different effect. Millenarian beliefs traditionally revolve around an expectation of the end of the world. In fact, such attitudes have a certain fine logic. If you had imposed the constraints of a particular belief upon the flow of time then you had to assume that they would operate. It made sense to expect the end of the world in AD 1000. Interestingly, we do the opposite now, for the most part. Attention focuses not on a full stop, but on what comes next. What will this millennium bring? I suppose that I should be speculating about the future of the book, let alone the future of fiction. My own bet is that both will do nicely, at least for the foreseeable future. I have served for the last six years on the Board of the British Library, repository for a national and global archive and also nowadays, necessarily, at the cutting edge of information technology. The director of that area of the Library's activities, himself something of a cutting-edge man, was asked recently what technological innovation he would most like to have been responsible for. His answer was: the book. The most lasting and efficient information device going: portable, user-friendly, not dependent on any external support system. The book will be with us for a long while yet. But what about fiction?

I am a writer of fiction. I am also an agnostic. I subscribe to a set of moral standards which are not fundamentally different from those central to Christianity, but I cannot believe in a deity or in an afterlife. And I have come to believe that in an age when most art is secular, and when formal religious belief is probably rare among novelists, there is an eerie affinity between religious conviction and the writing of fiction. It is my purpose in this essay to try to investigate and discuss this affinity. I think that first of all we have to define what it is that writers of serious fiction are trying to do. And immediately this becomes an impossible task, because of course they are a volatile and disparate lot – multilingual, multicultural and quite properly without common purpose or aim. All you can say with accuracy is that each is purveying a vision and interpretation of the world which is unique, and that is why we need many writers of fiction. But, that said, I think it is possible to find some more precise objectives or at least qualities of most fiction, whether it be the novel or the short story.

The Nature of Fiction

Narrative, as such, is subject to the winds of literary fashion. At some points story is the very essence of fiction; at others it is profoundly unrespectable and to be disguised or discarded. But even when that is the case there is structure and there is order. Situations and characters have been carefully chosen, a language has been found with which to create a particular atmosphere, suggest a particular climate. There is order. There is an internal coherence, the absence of which we quickly notice in an unsuccessful piece of fiction. 'It doesn't work,' we say, when searching for what it is that is inadequate. We feel we have been sold short. So . . . even while it may reject narrative as such, fiction seeks to impose order and create structure. And to what end? Well, to present a particular vision of the world, certainly. There the common purpose comes to a halt. The vision may be a cautionary and political one – an Orwellian vision. It may be some majestic discussion of the nature of evil by Dostoyevsky or William Golding. Or it may have the less ambitious but no less valid or valuable intention of creating a fictional reflection of the real world which illuminates and entertains. This is what most fiction sets out to do, and is none the worse for it. I certainly read to be entertained. But I read for more than that as well – I go to fiction for illumination, for enlightenment. To be made to think. I go to fiction to escape the prison of my own concerns, to experience the fresh air of someone else's imaginative outlook. Of course, any writer is a part of the process whereby literature is itself a narrative – books beget books. I am influenced – whether in a negative or a positive sense – by everything I have ever read. I shall come back to this point later. For the moment, I shall take a look at the role of fiction. I cannot believe that this need for story, for fable, on the part of both readers and writers, is going to evaporate. The forms that fiction takes undoubtedly will change – fiction is the most mutable of literary forms and is re-worked by each generation of writers. And its significance will change too – people will seek different satisfactions, but stories, as such, will survive. Let us consider the ancestry of fiction.

Fiction has become, I suppose, the form of art most widely familiar. Everyone, or pretty nearly everyone, reads some form of fiction at some point, even if it is only pulp fiction bought to read on the tube or while lying on a beach. And why does it have this universal appeal? What is it that people seek in a story? It seems

Penelope Lively

to me that fiction provides two distinct satisfactions, and that it does so at every level; there is indeed a common denominator, of a kind, a quality that in an eerie way links the contemporary blockbuster with the most profound and thoughtful novel. We read for escape, for enlargement of our own horizons, in search of the experiences that are not likely to come our way. And we read for identification, to find reflected in fictional form, transmuted by someone else's vision, the things that have happened to us – a through-the-looking-glass version of our own emotions, our own problems and pleasures. Popular fiction supplies the need in a basic and businesslike way – at its best with a curious innocence, at worst with commercial cynicism. Adventure, romance, sex, money – the fantasy worlds that supply an antidote to the deficiencies of the one in which people actually live.

What we call serious fiction does not enjoy wide patronage. But it flourishes; those who do care about it evidently care quite a lot. All the same, they are a minority. It is sobering to note that out of the 100 authors most frequently borrowed from public libraries, according to the Public Lending Right returns, a tiny handful only would be generally classified as literary novelists. I find this puzzling. Why is it that once fiction has taken the crucial step from superficial to serious intention it then becomes inaccessible, or uninteresting, to most readers, because although the divide is a crucial one, it is also a subtle one? Most so-called serious fiction looks much the same, at a cursory glance, as most popular fiction. It has characters, dialogue and, most probably, a narrative of some sort. And it is still supplying, in a general sense, those two primary requirements I mentioned earlier – it enlarges the reader's experience and it also confirms it. But there is a further ingredient – the added dimension of authorial involvement. The writer, too, is now in search of something, is using fiction as a means of exploring and developing personal preoccupations, of trying to provide explanations and interpretations of human conduct, and to reflect upon the human condition. I think it is this element of authorial need and intention which divides serious from popular fiction, and moves a novel onto that plane at which it is both satisfying those two simple and elemental requirements but also challenging the reader with the offer of an interpretation of the world. The sophisticated reader will then reject that interpretation, accept it, or quarrel with it according to taste. This is the point at which fiction has ceased to be mere entertainment and has become part of the landscape of the imagination. It has affected the way in which the reader sees the world.

Fiction and the Ordering of our World

If I am trying to get an insight into a society, whether it is removed from my own in time or in space, I go to its fiction. I think that the way into the nineteenth-century mind is through its literature (though, I hasten to say, I was trained as a historian and have an absolute belief also in the value of historical knowledge and historical context). I believe that there is a narrative process within literature itself, an interdependence, but I am deeply suspicious of the notion that so-called texts are free-floating concepts, the study of which is tarnished by an insistence on context and temporality. I think that writers spring from particular circumstances, are conditioned by them and write out of them. An aspect of this conditioning is, of course, what they happen to read as well as where and how they happen to live – a novelist writes out of literary affinity or aversion, whether unconsciously or deliberately. But above all he or she writes out of a social and historical climate, and bears witness to it.

As we all know, the novel as a fictional form was born in the eighteenth century. That is not strictly accurate, because there are precursors and maverick appearances elsewhere in time and space, but it will do as a general statement. But fiction itself was old by then. There has always been fiction, ever since some shaman figure of deep antiquity first reached for a form of narrative allegory to attract the attention of the tribe around the fireside. Allegory, myth, legend, folklore – the earliest forms of fiction tell a story, but they set out to do a great deal more than that. Here, above all, we have the literature of explanation and interpretation, the literature in which people seek to find and state a meaning for the world they see around them and the circumstances in which they find themselves. All people have produced their own creation myths, their own grand fictional accounts of how the world began, how we came into it, how to account for the rising and setting of the sun, and the annual regeneration of life. It has never been enough, even in the simplest of societies, just to observe these things and go about the daily business. Always, there are the mythologies, the cosmic stories, the cast of gods and spirits, the heroic human players. The stories grow in interest and complexity as societies become more sophisticated. The most abiding of them – the narratives of the Old Testament, the content of Greek and Norse mythology – have coloured our imaginations ever since and are inextricably interwoven with our prose and poetry, a network of allusion that must make a great deal of European literature disturbingly incomprehensible to generations not familiar with the language of the Bible and of classical myth and legend. The night sky is peopled with the heroic figures of antiquity – Perseus, Orion, Cassiopeia, Andromeda; the intricate calculations and observations of today's astronomers perpetuate the most ancient fictions.

First, account for the world; then, account for the human condition and human behaviour. After mythology – folklore and fairy-tale. This is the fiction of moral recommendation and of consolation, the interpretation of the collective plight devised by and for generations of peasantry. The world is a cruel place. Life is short, and governed by the malign hand of fate. The rich and the bad tend to prosper, while the poor, the weak and the good go to the wall. Can this be right? Of course not, say the stories. And they set out to create an ideal world in which things happen as they ought to happen: tyrants, misers and wicked stepmothers receive their come-uppance; the humble triumph over the elevated, frogs turn into princes, dry leaves into gold, and the youngest son gets the girl. It is a distorting mirror of the real world, and full of satisfaction for the disgruntled listener who has perceived only too clearly that there is outrage all around, that misery is rife, that human conduct is despicable, that force rules and that you can rely on nothing. Not so, say the stories. There is another world and another code, a world in which people like you flourish and virtue receives its reward. Fiction has again, but differently, supplied a palliative and an account.

Today, we see fairy-stories as fit only for children. Perhaps in fact it is only the children who are fit for fairy-stories, who are in that condition of anarchical innocence that enables them to see the world for what it is, and are appropriately appalled. We are acclimatized, and either adjust, endure or try to make what improvements are possible by means of political activity. Children are still in a condition of original outrage, meeting up with instability and unfairness at every turn, and responding naturally to the consoling ethic of fairy-stories, which incidentally do a great deal more even than that for the psychological health of the child, though there is not time here to expand on that interesting topic. Suffice it to say that children understand the meaning of fairy-stories probably rather better than we do, or, indeed, supply their own meaning.

Fiction as a Narrative Process

I return at this point, briefly, to a question I raised earlier – the sense in which fiction is itself a narrative process, that books beget books, that all writers, however maverick or innovative they may consider themselves, work within a cumulative structure. The house of fiction has many rooms. Form and content are the stuff of literary criticism – how writers write or should write, and what they should be writing about. On a different level, any reader of Sunday newspapers will have noted that many reviewers spend much of their time attacking novelists for not having written an entirely different kind of book. But, disparate and contentious as the literary world may be, it is still one in which mutual indebtedness abounds. Writers learn from aversion quite as much as from affinity. The winds of fashion blow strong, and may blow authors off the scene altogether, but the shrewder assessments of the long-term view have a way of sorting things out, of sifting the significant from the standard contribution, and even, come to that, allowing the standard contribution its place in the scheme of things. And what is most important is that all of it is inter-dependent, if only in terms of rejection and regeneration. There is another structure here, another narrative – that in which the art is continually seeking its own definition, its own ideal expression.

The novel as we recognize it was born in the eigh-teenth century, in the age of enlightenment and of scepti-cism. It seems to me that this was no accident. Fiction offers structure and a vision of life, whatever else it may offer along the way, and however far it may depart from the concepts of narrative and of a realistic reflection of the society from which it springs. I am not suggesting that the novel as a form was provoked by scepticism or denial of Christian belief; some of the great works of fiction address themselves to central issues from within the assumptions of religious faith. Most eighteenth- and nineteenth-century novelists would have subscribed to Christian belief. But they were writing in an age of doubt, with traditional certainties questioned and supplanted in the new light of reason and scientific investigation. Fiction is frequently neither reasonable nor scientific, but successful fiction offers a satisfying internal coherence, an order, a structure, and, moreover, it turns a searchlight upon the world and tries to investigate and comment upon the human plight. Here was a secular form of allegory for an increasingly secular society.

Fiction and Unbelief and Fate

At this point I need to abandon the novel for a moment and look at the plight of the agnostic, the atheist, the non-believer, because I think that it is indeed a plight. I call myself an agnostic, which implies inability to believe in a deity, rather than outright rejection of the very concept of a deity. I know that I can't believe in a god, and why I can't, but I accept that others can, respect their reasons for so doing without accepting them, and feel a curious combination of envy and wonder at the solaces available to them which are not available to me. The Iranian earthquake of 1990 and the many deaths incurred therein were described by a Muslim religious leader as an act of God and accepted as such. Of course, he could not logically say anything else, and he was probably wise to make no further comment. Believers will deal with this knowledge in their own way and we are irresistibly reminded of 1755, of the Lisbon earthquake and of Voltaire's famous engagement with the problem of evil. Here is the great stumbling block for any agnostic – or rather, one of the two great stumbling blocks, the other being the question of creation, which I will get on to shortly. How can the existence of God be reconciled with the prevalence of evil – with man's inhumanity to man and with the malign hand of fate? 'Is He willing to prevent evil but not able to do so? Then is He impotent? Is He able but not willing? Then is He malevolent? Is He both able and willing? Whence, then, is evil?'

It is the theodicy question, I suppose, the problem of evil, which is the issue most vigorously responsible for the creation of unbelievers, both historically and individually. Christianity has its answers, of course, rooted in the arguments about original sin and the imperative of an imperfect world in which man may exercise his capacity for moral choice. This is not the time nor the occasion to air the debate. My discussion here is not about who is right, or whether God exists, but about art and religion, about fiction and religion, and I am trying to make the point that the novel, with its characteristics of artificial order and of query, may perhaps be the form of art which has appealed to many people as appropriate in the increasingly secular society of the last 200 years. Indeed it sprang into life in the age when thinking men and women were first expressing dissatisfaction with the certainties of received dogma both widely and energetically. Fiction has been a vehicle for the discussion of the nature of man from *Robinson Crusoe* to *Lord of the Flies*; allegory is as powerful a form as it has ever been. Great novels have addressed themselves to the great themes, have examined and tried to explain why people behave as they do but also, whether explicitly or implicitly, have always confronted and considered the other perennial problem, both for believers and agnostics – that of the unacceptability of fate.

We lead private lives which are subject to the dictation of public events. We believe that we make choices in life, but know that our range of choice is defined for us by circumstance. We know, too, that we owe the fortune or misfortune of our appearance and our constitution to the cumulative legacy of our genes. We go to bed at night certain that the sun will rise again the next day but without any certainty that we will rise with it. We have to confront the fact that it is only up to a point that we dispose of our lives, and that even in the relatively airy climate of a politically stable Western society history may choose to pick us off tomorrow, or the proverbial bus may be waiting for us to step off the pavement. Mostly we do the sensible and expedient thing and we don't think about it too much: 'Human kind cannot bear very much reality.'[1] But when we do we are outraged, both by our own impotence and by the messiness of arbitrary fate. Is this really all that there is to life? An obstacle race from the cradle to the grave, with the prizes going to those who picked a high number in the lottery. Apparently so, and understandably enough most people find this an unacceptable state of affairs and look for solace, most usually in religion.

But for those unable to accept such an explanation or consolation the problem remains. It is the price we pay for sentient life, for being thinking creatures. And what does all this have to do with fiction? I am back with the question of structure. In real life, the choices available are limited, though they are indeed there. What happens to us is determined by a combination of hazard and decision – a terrifying process, if you stop to think about it, which is of course why for the most part we do not. The novelist, on the other hand, does nothing but make choices. There is no hazard in a novel, or at least there ought not to be. The whole thing is an artificial construct, a confection of characters and situations created to put across a particular vision of the world, a fraudulent landscape and a mendacious tale to act as the vehicle for the novelist's version of the truth about the world as he or she sees it. And the whole thing rests on a multiplicity of intricate, careful and considered choices. The novelist chooses what to put in and, most crucially, what to leave out – any novel is a sequence of omissions. The novelist leaves out all that is extraneous to the purpose of the book – all that the characters may do, think or say which is not relevant to the matter in hand. Real life is a very different business, for any of us – a confusion of plots and narratives all running concurrently and at different stages of development. The novelist, having chosen the characters and designed for them personalities which suit the purpose of the novel, then sets about eliminating all those aspects of their lives which are irrelevant to the central

89

issue of the book. If the story is one of matrimonial mayhem and family tensions we will probably be told nothing about the current international situation or the economic climate. If the focus is on drug-running and the Mafia we may not hear a great deal about the central figure's relationship with his mother or his views on contemporary political issues.

Fiction, then, might seem to be the antithesis of life as it is, in fact, lived. It depends upon order and structure, where life is disordered and unstructured. It is the product of unfettered choice – or at least of choice that is fettered only by the individual novelist's creative ability; in that sense too it is quite unlike real life. Is it perhaps this quality of life-through-the-looking-glass that gives fiction its fascination? I believe that it is, and that the need of it is innate in most people and is demonstrated by every child who falls silent to listen to a story, responding instinctively to that marriage of a structure and an interpretation which is so manifestly missing from its own experience.

Fiction: A Response to the Contingent

And what about the writers? What do they get out of it? At this point I have to speak for myself alone, because that is all that I can do. And in order to give some idea of that I take refuge for a moment in palaeontology, a subject of which I have only the most amateur knowledge but by which I am fascinated.

In British Columbia, high in the Canadian Rockies, there is a unique and remarkable fossil bed known as the

Burgess Shale. The Burgess Shale is Middle Cambrian – of great antiquity even in palaeontological terms, some 500 million years old – and the special quality of this quarry is that it has produced a harvest of tiny fossils encountered nowhere else in the world and prompting some extraordinary and provocative conclusions about the history of life on this planet and the ancestry of Homo sapiens. There is an assembly of animals so bizarre that they appear to have stepped straight out of Walt Disney's *Fantasia*, or a science fiction extravaganza. There is a creature like an animated hairbrush, there is a miniature swimming doormat, there is an object with five eyes and a vacuum-cleaner nozzle and another which looks for all the world like a feather duster. There are creatures with stilts in place of legs, others with frills and one that looks like a lotus flower. Many of them are beautiful; all of them are startling. But what gives scientists pause for thought is that among this array of creatures, which includes representatives of the ancestors of all the four major groups of arthropods, the dominant animals on earth today; along with these recognizable versions of species we know, there are also 20 to 30 kinds of arthropods which cannot be placed in any modern group. In other words, the Burgess Shake offers a diversity of designs beyond the wildest imaginings, nearly all of which have been wiped off the face of the earth. And amid this exotic gallery there is an inoffensive and not especially interesting-looking slug-like animal called *Pikaia*. *Pikaia* is a chordate, a primitive form of vertebrate, our ancestor.

Now what is exciting and provocative about all this,

for palaeontologists and indeed for anyone – certainly for me – is that it is a demonstration not only of the operation of contingency in the evolutionary process, but of the way in which human existence is itself the product of contingency. Evolution is the effect of innumerable small adjustments in biological develop-ment, not accidental but responding to environment and circumstance, each contingent upon the previous one. To peer into the remote biological past by way of the fossil record is to perceive and to be duly awed by the odds against the particular set of contingent events that has led to the evolution of Homo sapiens as the domi-nant and sentient species. It is not just that it might not have been thus, but that the dice are so heavily loaded against it being thus.

I find this both a sobering thought and a provocative one. There is also a gratifying symmetry about the way in which it imitates our own experience of what happens in an individual lifecycle – a sequence of adjustments of personality and personal action in response to circum-stance and environment. Some of us, of course, are given rather more opportunity to negotiate than others. I believe it was the Hollywood actress Sophie Tucker who used to proclaim: 'I've been poor and I'v been rich, and believe me, rich is better.' Those who are well equipped – financially, physically, intellectually – have more potential for manipulation of the pack of cards they have been dealt than do others. Life's struggle looks rather less daunting from a New York penthouse than from a Bombay slum. But, whoever or whatever we are, contin-gency remains the dominating factor. One thing happens because another did; we follow one path rather than another, or rather than an infinite multiplicity of other paths. Our lives are littered with dead ends, or not so much with dead ends as with roads that vanish into the shadows, peopled with those we never met and leading into landscapes we never visited. This is in its way as disturbing as contemplation of the random effects of fate.

I am sobered by the notion of contingency. But as a novelist I find it both provocative and entirely familiar. I am on home-ground. This is the tool of my trade. Each time that I start to plan a novel I am juggling with calculation and contingency, setting in motion a chain of circumstances each of which depends closely upon all that has come before. The circumstances may or may not be a narrative in the conventional sense, but if I have paid insufficient attention to the sequence of information given to the reader, if I have left unexplained gaps or taken awkward turns, then the final product will be unsatisfactory. It won't work. It will lack internal coherence and the reader will be uncomfortable and dissatisfied. Each step of the book, each paragraph, each page, must arise from all that went before, and ought to arise effortlessly and apparently naturally, as though any other outcome were unthinkable. That is art imitating nature.

The Mystery of Creation

The question of creation is, of course, the other great stumbling block for the agnostic. How and why do human beings exist? And one form of the straight scientific answer would be – because that unimposing slug-like creature *Pikaia* survived the decimation of the Cambrian period rather than the hairbrush, the nozzle and the feather duster. And in a post-Darwinian age I don't imagine that many Christians would deny that, or would put forward the argument from design, which is actually one I am rather fond of if only for the evocative nature of its best-known expression by the eighteenth-century theologian William Paley. Paley said: 'Suppose I were crossing a heath and I stubbed my foot against a stone, and you asked me how the stone got there, I would probably reply – "No doubt it has always been there".' 'But suppose,' he said, 'I were to stumble upon a watch instead, and were asked the same question, I should hardly give the same answer. Such is the intricacy of design of the watch that one must suppose that it has been made by someone, and for a purpose.' I have to say that at this point my narrative instinct takes over and I too start to wonder where the watch came from. It is one of those eighteenth-century fob watches, I assume, and undoubtedly it was dropped by this high-wayman who was lurking on the heath in anticipation of the 11.15 coach, and in order to check that it had not already passed he took out the watch – which incidentally he had hefted from William Pitt the week before – at which point his horse suddenly reared . . . Enough. The watch is a purely metaphysical watch, offered by a late eighteenth-century mind to us in order to serve as the basis for the argument that the complexity of the natural world demands that it cannot have arisen other than by design, and must therefore have had a designer.

Well, since 1859 and the publication of Darwin's *The Origin of Species* we have known that while Paley was quite right to draw attention to the complexity of the natural world, this complexity is the result of natural selection, an unconscious and automatic process which is the explanation for our existence and that of every other living organism, and which has no purpose or objective, but simply operates.

The problem of evil is insurmountable. I do not find the absence of a Creator disturbing in the same way. The beauty and intricacy of the physical world, and the elegance of the evolutionary process, are quite enough. I do not need there to be a purpose or a divine force behind it. The difficulty, for me, lies with our own relationship to it all – or rather, with our absence of relationship. The natural world is impervious; it neither knows nor cares. It performs a mindless cycle of death and regeneration. And here are we, in the midst of it, martyrs to emotion, irrational and superstitious, in a perpetual state of confusion about the role of sun, stars, moon, rivers and hills, tree, rock and grass. We start out propitiating them, aware of our dependence, scared that if we do not do the right thing the sun will fail to rise, the water to flow, the seasons to progress. And when eventually we have acquired some confidence in the stability of things we become exercised about this disturbing absence of rapport, the insensitivity of our surroundings, and we start to anthropomorphize rather differently. We attribute human response and emotion to other species or to the landscape – the pathetic fallacy of literature. And the crux of the matter is the challenge of this same complexity and elegance – are we to see it as a solace or a mockery? There is the world, looking as it does, functioning as it does, permanent and entirely unresponsive; here we are, sentient and caring, and entirely impermanent. What are we to feel about this?

It is the dilemma of intelligence, again. We are the only species to have achieved this condition of perpetual anxiety about destiny and origins. It is the price we pay, and a further price is a collective amnesia about our own pasts. The accretions of experience, whether personal experience or tribal experience, make it impossible to recover the anarchic visions of ignorance – of two kinds of ignorance, the ignorance of childhood and the ignorance of early man.

The Questioning Nature of Fiction

I am getting towards my conclusion, and am very conscious of having flown a number of kites – too many, I dare say – and of having asked a lot of questions but provided no answers. That, I'm afraid, is what most novelists do. And it is vital that they should do so. I have been trying to investigate the affinity between fiction and religion. I have not set out to make a case for fiction as some form of anti-religion, as some form of religious substitute. That would be both arrogant and unrealistic – arrogant because it would be to claim for literature a constituency which it has never had, and unrealistic because it would be to expect too much of the palliative effect of literature. My case is that what fiction has done and can do is to furnish meaning and order where neither are apparent, and furthermore to furnish an infinite variety of meanings and forms of order, to ask endless questions and propose a wealth of interpretations. It enables us to share the vision of others. It gives us seven-league boots with which to step beyond the boundaries of time and of space, and in that sense it is a far more effective form of cultural and temporal communication than the newspaper, the aircraft and the Internet.

Let me end on a personal note. I am continually surprised that people read my fiction. I am glad that they do – a writer writes, after all, in order to communicate – but I am also daunted. It brings home to me the significance of what I am attempting. My engagement with fiction is first and foremost as a reader, and it has had a great deal to do with my agnosticism and with the doubts and questionings attendant upon absence of belief. Though, that being said, I am well aware that doubts and questionings are equally attendant upon faith. My point is that a lifetime of reading fiction has provided me with a landscape of the mind for which I am profoundly grateful, because it is not exclusively my own. Its furnishings are eclectic and exotic, and I owe them to the imaginings of others. Reading fiction has not provided me with answers, but it has taught me to ask questions, and never to be satisfied with a single explanation.

Notes

1. T. S. Eliot, Burnt Norton, Part 1, in *The Four Quartets*, in *The Complete Poems and Plays of T. S. Eliot*, (London: Faber, 1969), p. 172.

David Jones and the Elusive Memory

RICHARD MARSH

Setting the Scene

The helicopter flew low over the mountains until the ground dropped away to the arable plain. From the windows, our first sight was of burning houses. We could see four or five at a glance. As we passed low over farms and hamlets, children who were playing in the backyards waved at our aircraft. Finally, in the gathering gloom, we set our aircraft down, spiralling out of the sky on to a football field. Met by our escorts, we climbed into our transports and headed through the pockmarked and damaged town, and then out along a wooded valley. The rain began, stair-rods beating down hard on the top of the vehicle, darkening the evening. Finally, we reached the monastery, like so many holy places, nestling in a valley by a river. We were greeted gracefully, if not warmly, by the few monks left within and we made our way to our rooms under the gaze of hard-faced men and women clustered around the gatehouse. By now it was late, and we had been travelling all day. All that was left to us was some conversation with the bishop, a scratch supper and then the hope of sleep. And the rain fell, and from the town, we heard the not-too-distant sound of machine-gun fire.

Sleep was disturbed – outside in the monastery courtyard a woman keened throughout the night. Delivered to the monastery by Italian forces as we arrived, she was the last surviving inhabitant of her village and the night before she had been tied up and made to watch as her daughter was raped and then killed, before the village was set alight. Her daughter had been laid to rest behind the monastery church, but not in the graveyard. For on the slopes of the idyllic valley were snipers, and the graveyard, with its many mounds of newly turned earth, lay in the direct line of fire.

As we spoke in the silver light of a damp dawn, our encounter embraced a certain timelessness. The face of the woman – a Serb in the wrong place, at the wrong time – tear-streaked and pinched with fear, was the face of the century and perhaps of all centuries. But here in Kosovo her emblematic status seemed somehow heightened. She was symbolic of something greater and more awesome than herself and her sad personal tragedy. In a sense she was iconic of all refugees, all mothers, all the dispossessed and all those whose misery has come about through the intractable weight of memory, cleaving human beings one from another.

Some miles to the north there is another valley lined by a fine city and across the river, bridges – some of more notoriety than others. I walked on one of them a few months ago much as I had walked on it many times, trying to imagine the scene as an Archduke crossed it and a young man seized his opportunity and fired a shot or two. For this was Sarajevo.

Still further to the north, a few years earlier still at the beginning of a war, and my memory took me to an elegant house in a Belgrade suburb where one chilly winter's night we sat drinking slivovitz and talking. And through the windows we saw the snow and the UNHCR aid trucks mustering to take their convoys into Bosnia. The Archbishop, whose house it was, and who brewed his own most excellent slivovitz, its bottles decorated with his own name and coat of arms, reminded us that we were sitting in what had been the main drawing-room of the Austro-Hungarian embassy. It was here that the report of those shots on the bridge in Sarajevo turned itself into a declaration of war. The Russian ambassador, in his haste to stop a precipitous act, had a heart attack and died in the doorway, and so was unleashed a war which, despite the high-blown rhetoric which surrounds it – the War to end all wars – remains in many ways a conundrum and a question even for us now as we begin a new century and a new millennium.

David Jones and the Great War

Those who signed the declaration of war in that house in Belgrade, still less the young student who fired the shots, could have little idea of the real consequences of their actions or that, many hundreds of miles away, a young man named David Jones, from Brockley in London, would find himself impelled to join a ragbag regiment of London Welsh and experience the vicissitudes of what he called 'the disciplines of the wars'. He appears to have been a shy, unprepossessing sort of a bloke; he was the son of a Welsh printer's overseer whose mother was the daughter of a mast- and block-maker from Rotherhithe. Before the First World War he had briefly attended Camberwell College of Art in London but in 1915 he joined up and became a private in the Royal Welsh Fusiliers (London Battalion). For a gawkishly shy young man of artistic sensibilities army life and war must have come as something of a shock. But he seems to have adapted to it well, if ineptly. A few of his pencil sketches of basic training and of life in the trenches remain, although Jones himself was deeply contemptuous of them as 'art school stuff'. But it is his long prose poem account of the period between 1915 and the middle of 1916 which he published in 1937 which perhaps shows more readily the massive impact that the war was to have upon him.

In his introduction to the poem he explained his slightly curious choice of title, *In Parenthesis* having something of a gnomic quality about it. And he did so in the rambling, round about sort of writing that characterizes both his poetry and his prose:

This writing is called *In Parenthesis* because I have written it in a kind of space between – I don't know between quite what – but as you turn aside to do something; and because for us amateur soldiers (and especially for the writer, who was not only amateur, but grotesquely incompetent, a knocker-over of piles, a parade's despair) the war itself was a parenthesis – how glad we thought we were to step outside its brackets at the end of '18 – and also because our curious type of existence here is altogether in parenthesis.[1]

Perhaps because *In Parenthesis* is the product of a long period of gestation during which Jones abandoned his childhood low church Anglicanism for the Roman Catholic Church, and in the course of which he was to come under the spell of Eric Gill, *In Parenthesis* has a very different, more discursive quality to it than the work of many other more well-known war-poets. Although it is not without its lyric qualities, his treatment of those months is more extended, its episodic narrative flow punctuated with telling vignettes of army and trench life: for instance, the following passage from early in the book, where Jones describes the period of waiting experienced by himself and his comrades behind the trenches in France before they reached the front:

In a place of scattered farms and the tranquillity of fields, in a rest area many miles this side of the trench system; a place unmolested and untouched so far, by the actual shock of men fighting. They did short route marches each day along winding ways saturated with continued rain. They did platoon-drill and arm-drill in soggy fields behind their billets.

They were given lectures on very wet days in the barn, with its great roof, sprung, unpreaching, humane, and redolent of a vanished order. Lectures on military tactics that would be more or less commonly understood. Lectures on hygiene, by the medical officer, who was popular, who glossed his technical discourses with every lewdness, whose heroism and humanity reached towards sanctity.

One day the Adjutant addressed them on the history of the Regiment. Lectures by the Bombing Officer: he sat in the straw, a mild young man, who told them lightly of the efficacy of his trade; he predicted an important future for the new Mills Mk. IV grenade, just on the market; he discussed the improvised jam-tins of the veterans, of the bombs of after the Marne, grenades of Loos and Lavengie – he compared these elementary, amateurish, inefficiencies with the compact and supremely satisfactory invention of this Mr Mills, to whom his country was so greatly indebted.[2]

And here, almost in microcosm, we have a snapshot of David Jones's art. Much that was written either during or after the First World War stressed the negation of individuality, the soldier as cog in a machine. Although David Jones himself acknowledged that there was a change in the war, after the period recorded in *In Parenthesis* when things 'hardened into a more relentless, mechanical affair, it took on a more sinister aspect. The wholesale slaughter of the later years, the conscripted levies filling the gaps in every file of four, knocked the bottom out of the intimate, continuing, domestic life of small contingents of men, within whose structure Roland could find, and, for a reasonable while, enjoy, his Oliver' (p. ix). But Jones chooses to record a time of war where the individual was valued and with him the grace of comradeship, and this description is not, I think, a failure, nor is it a resort to obscurantism or romanticism. Rather, it is an honest evocation of Jones's actual experience. Throughout his painting and his written work, Jones places an immense value on what he describes in his preface to his second great poem *The Anathemata*, as 'the actually loved and known'.

The Mythological Power of Religion

At the beginning of their 'parenthesis', that stepping away from normality which will change normality itself, the soldiers sit in the barn which Jones describes with the sorts of registers of language with which you might describe a church. Indeed, Jones's conversion to Catholicism opened up for him a whole new world of symbols and images which he saw reflected in the world around him. For his was an elusive and shape-shifting world, full of connections and amplifications and, above all, connections to the past. Throughout his work David Jones relies on and engages with the cultural heritage of Western European Christianity, especially its Roman and Celtic forms; all the ideas which lie close to the heart of his work are either explicitly religious or have immense implications for those who would think about God. For example, Jones's description of the doling out of the rum ration:

> Dispense salvation,
> Strictly apportion it,
> let us taste and see,

let us be renewed,
For christ's sake let us be warm.
O have a care – don't spill the precious,
O don't jog his hand – ministering:
do take care.
O please – give the poor bugger elbow room.[3]

Here Jones's depiction of a welcome everyday event in the lives of the soldiers has all the quality of a description of a priest dispensing the elements at the Eucharist. Or perhaps we have got it the wrong way round? Is Jones's intuition right? Or is the distribution at the Eucharist a reflection of something more profoundly and gratuitously human? It matters little, except that by raising to the eyeglass of our consciousness something so mundane through this profound yet lucid examination, the role itself is somehow changed and our perception of it deepened.

David Jones in a sense, and a very good sense, 'mythologizes' the experience of those who went to war with him. And here we need to be careful, for myth, like language itself, is slippery and elusive stuff, all too open to cack-handed and facile interpretation. George Steiner reminds us that:

A mythology crystallizes sediments accumulated over great stretches of time. It gathers into conventional form the primal memories and historical experience of the race. Being the speech of the mind when it is in a state of wonder and perception, the great myths are elaborated as slowly as language itself.[4]

Richard Marsh

Myth and Memory

Many writers and poets of this century have found themselves attracted to the deposits of faith or to those
deposits of myth bequeathed to them from the Greek,
Latin and Celtic worlds. Eliot and Yeats are just two
examples of this. But Jones's use of the idea of myth
has its own particularity or specificity. In an essay
entitled 'The Myth of Arthur' he wrote:

> To conserve, to develop, to bring together, to make
> significant for the present what past holds, without
> dilution or any deleting, but rather by understanding
> and transubstantiating the material, this is the func-
> tion of genuine myth, neither pedantic nor popularis-
> ing, nor indifferent to scholarship but saying always
> 'of these thou hast given me have I lost none'.[5]

Genuine myth is specific and yet inclusive. Its form has
a transparency by means of which the truth may be seen
and appropriated. It is eternally significant, as is the
truth which it contains, and if within it the outward
form of truth is somehow transformed, transfigured and
transubstantiated, the essence of it is preserved intact.

It is not difficult to see how Jones understood myth
to be wedded to the whole business of poetry, painting
and the making of things. The form in which the ancient
deposits were given, or handed on, is of the most profound significance, as also is the sense that myths grasp
at a reality or a truth at which historical facts cannot
attempt to grasp. It is a core of undiluted signifying

presence conveyed in the shape of story lying beyond formulation and within, yet beyond even history, which interests him and which enables him to slide so eloquently between the Christian and pagan mythic heritage.

The intimate details of trench life experienced by Jones and his comrades, even the language that they speak – cockney slang, Welsh and that rich seam of Welsh-English – become for him a window through which the soldiers are seen as bearing within themselves the whole history of their race. So when one of the soldiers, nicknamed Dai Great-coat, utters a long boast associating himself with all the soldiers of the foretime, in the manner of boasts to be found in Welsh poetry, somehow the meaninglessness and murk of trench warfare takes on a new resonance.

This Dai adjusts his slipping shoulder heightened straps, wraps close his misfit outsize greatcoat – he articulates his English with an alien care:

My fathers were with the Black Prinse of Wales
at the passion of
The blind Bohemian king.
They served in these fields,
it is in the histories that you can read it, Corporal –
    boys
Gower, they were – it is writ down – yes.
        Wot about Methuselum, Taffy?
I was with Abel when his brother found him
under the green tree.

I built a shit-house for Artaxerxes.
I was the spear in Balin's hand
        that made waste King Pellam's land.
I took the smooth stones of the brook,
I was with Saul playing before him.
I saw him armed like Derfel Gatheren.[6]

And so on through the myths and legends which Jones sees as integral to the identity of the 'white isles of the Britons'. Dai, the universal soldier, even includes himself among the soldiers at Christ's crucifixion and before that he claims to have been 'in Michael's trench when bright Lucifer bowled his primal salient out'. But the boast ends where it began in the trench with the salutary reminder that 'Old soljers never die, they simply fade away'. Here the mythic meanders of Dai Great-coat bridge the gap between contemporary experience of time both sacred and profane. He makes a partial map of this difficult territory, in many respects limited, and yet, paradoxically capable of encapsulating an almost infinite amount of information. Although he rejected the idea of being a mystic, Jones's view of the world is certainly of a place which is shot through with the sacred. He is a keen-eyed observer, with a sharp ear for resonance and allusion, for the here and now, for the actually loved and known – these become windows onto something much greater. Something to which humanity, responding to its vocation to be sign-making, needs to respond.

Myth, Memory, Mass and Sign

I have already described the way in which eucharistic images are used by Jones to enrich and draw out the significance of the mundane doling out of the rum ration. This points us towards what is, for David Jones, absolutely crucial. The myth or narrative by which all other narratives and myths are to be interpreted – and, in a sense, from which they all flow – is the Christian 'myth' of the death and Resurrection of Jesus Christ.

Throughout his life, Jones argued that humanity's very nature involves the making of things, the creation of art, things sufficient of themselves and owing no explanation for their being: to use Jones's own terms, these are things which are 'gratuitous' or 'inutile' rather than 'utile' and 'technical'. Through this making, this assembly of signs and symbols, humanity stretches out of itself from the material and visible world towards reality, the ground of which is divine. 'A sign then must be significant of something, hence of some "reality", so of something "good"; so of something that is "sacred"'. If then, the art of sign-making is indicative of religion, then religion, and especially the Christian religion, is committed to art and the making of signs as a means of grace, and of articulation of the substance of that grace. This at the same time illuminates 'and grounds' the present reality and reaches further to 'other' sacred presence. So, when discussing Hogarth's painting *Shrimp Girl*, he is able to say: 'Here then is a *signum*, a made thing having such and such significance and totally independent of our fluctuating reactions or of our inability to react at all'.[7]

Central to all such sign-making is the Mass, which archetypally guarantees that events, and other things done, have a significance far beyond themselves; at the same time they may have an articulation which is also grounded in the physical and the practical. In the case of the Mass, its significance lies not in its making present the events of the Last Supper according to Dominical ordinance, but in its representation of the whole saving nexus of the Passion. David Jones read deeply and widely, and especially the works of both Dom Gregory Dix and the Jesuit, Maurice de la Taille. From the latter he derived a theological understanding of the Mass and the cross, centring on the matter of the sacrifice, which is the transference from the domain of the profane to that of the sacred. Between them Dix and de la Taille provided for Jones a eucharistic theology which linked the sign-making of the Mass and the redemptive centre of the Christian faith. Jesus, wrote de la Taille, 'placed himself in the order of signs'.

Moreover it was a theology which spilled over to inform and craft Jones's own thought on all art and sign making.[8] Human making of the Mass renders present the salvific sacrifice of the cross – and the cross itself is the guarantor of that sign-making. Rowan Williams has described Jones's reflections on 'art and Sacrament' as 'surely the best account in English this century of sacramental theology'.[9] His later poem *The Anathemata*, completed after the Second World War, is a lengthy meditation upon a historic journey through human history, arguing for the centrality of the Christian myth and its outworking in the celebration of the Eucharist. Gregory Dix's *The Shape of the Liturgy* concludes with an extended meditation on the ways that the Eucharist has been celebrated over time throughout the world:

> For century after century, spreading slowly to every continent and country and among every race on earth, this action has been done, in every conceivable human circumstance, for every conceivable human need from infancy and before it to extreme old age and after it, from the pinnacles of human greatness to the refuge of fugitives in the caves and dens of the earth.[10]

Indeed, *The Anathemata* could well be understood as a set of variations on Dix's purple passages. The poem opens with the image of the priest saying Mass in what Jones depicts as a late twentieth-century dystopic world in which religion, art and maybe even God are dead.

> We already and first of all discern him making this thing other. His groping syntax, if we attend, already shapes:
> ADSCRIPTAM, RATAM, RATIONABI-LEM . . . and by pre-application and for *them*, under modes and patterns altogether theirs, the holy and venerable hands lift up an efficacious sign.

> These, at the sagging end and chapter's close, standing humbly before the tables spread, in the apsidal houses, who intend life:

between the sterile ornaments
under the pasteboard baldachins
as, in the young-time, in the sap-years:
  between the living floriations
under the leaping arches.

(Ossific, trussed with ferric rods, the failing numina
of column and entablature, the genii of spire and tri-
forium, like great rivals met when all is done, nod
recognition across the cramped repeats of their dead
selves.)[11]

The rest of the poem develops these opening thoughts
and images in such a way that, at the end, when the
poet evokes for us a real death – that of Christ on the
Cross – and then returns us to the opening eucharistic
image, we are left not with the emptiness of the
beginning but with the glimmerings of hope. Between
the opening and the close the poet unfolds and connects
in a complex sinuous pattern, the elements of that hope;
the divine revelation of incarnation and the passion
together with the specific elements and instances of
human sign-making and artistry. This is a vision which
ranges over a canvas of huge proportions both geogra-
phical and historical, one which is conveyed in poetry
full of variation. Jones's world is one of constant transformation and allusion. Everything in it is very much
what it is and yet according to the discerning eye, has
infinitely more depth and richness. The significance of
everything that exists is not entirely dependent on itself
but on all that that has gone before. The world – for

Jones God's world – is in a state of constant transformation and transparency, and the past has particular significance for both the future and the present.

Myth, Modernity and Pessimism

Jones understood that the geomorphological processes that were at work in the making of physical landscape were mirrored in the life of cultures and civilizations; sediment lay upon sediment, and all was then twisted and assayed in the crucible of great foldings and eruptions of fire and ice. And, for the most part, he is able to hold all of this together through his passionate belief in the centrality of the Christian myth and its active presence within the Eucharist. But we must ask ourselves whether there is a romantic idealism here. Certainly, Jones asked the question himself, as he faced what we have come to know as the modern world. Increasing dependence on those things made in factories and the rule of machines, and the consequent distancing of that which is made from those who have made it, contributed in his mind at least, to an ever-deepening pessimism. Although Jones himself would see significance and importance in myths and legends expressed in richly textured language, a kind of magpie-like collector's ephemera, he was convinced that something profound had changed in the twentieth century.

> I have felt for His Wounds
> in nozzles and containers.
> I have wondered for the automatic devices.

I have tested the inane patterns
                    without prejudice.
I have been on my guard
                    not to condemn the unfamiliar.
For it is easy to miss Him
                    at the turn of a civilization.
   I have watched the wheels go round in case I
might see the living creatures like the appearance of
lamps, in case I might see the Living God projected
from the Machine. I have said to the perfected steel,
be my sister and for the glassy towers I thought I felt
some beginnings of His creature, but *A, a, a, Domine
Deus*, my hands found the glazed work unrefined and
the terrible crystal a stage-paste ... *Eia, Domine
Deus*.[12]

No longer, he feared, were the deposits of memory and
myth which he believed to be constitutive of identity
readily understood or valued. Even art itself was threat-
ened by the encroaching demands of technocracy.

Anamnesis and the Power of Memory

It might be tempting, in the face of this pessimism, to
write him off, but prophets are all too easy to ignore.
For David Jones understood the value of human remembering, the human process by which the mind actively
engages with the contents of memory. This is an activity
that takes up and deals with the things of the past, the
things of the present and those things which shape the
future. This is the crux of what Christians mean when

they talk about anamnesis – a word that should be used sparingly and certainly not carelessly or wantonly, for it is not a simple peering into the past. It is a recognition that remembering can be very powerful in shaping the present and the future. We break out of the constraints that living in a particular time and place press upon us – into a frame where past, present and future become flexibly intertwined. In anamnesis we have to face some truths which lie within human reach but which also challenge much human thought. The first of these truths is that despite our demonstrable finitude we have 'an immortal longing', a capacity to handle at least something of the infinite. The second truth is related to the first; the world that we experience as finite can be transcended and become the vehicle whereby the divine is revealed. In the context of the Christ-memory, the Church's memory, bread and wine are the essence of Christ himself – the divine condescension into the realm of human contingency; they become the constitutive memory of what was within the human apperception of what is, with the promise and hope of what will be. Jones understood this – he understood it because he had observed the moment where, at least in the West, people had begun to live under the illusion that the past had no enduring significance. And of course he was right, at least, up to a point. For although we may no longer value the deposits of human heritage there are many places in the world where the past is very much actively present in the daily lives of peoples, shaping the way that they look at the world and affecting the decisions that they make in all particulars.

This is the reason, after all, why I began this essay with a series of vignettes drawn from the Balkans – a part of the world where the past is very alive and terribly present.

The Bosnian novelist, Ivo Andric, in his book *The Bridge over the Drina*, paints a wonderful portrait of the history of a bridge in the town of Visegrad, from its building in the sixteenth century to its destruction in the twentieth. In doing so the bridge becomes a metaphor for something which holds together all the communities who use it – Muslim Bosnians, Serb Orthodox, Catholics and Jews – despite the tensions between them. But even he has to recognize that there were within these communities irreconcilable differences – even the children participate in this. The Serbs believe that a series of rounded hollows beside the bridge are the hoofmarks of Sarac, the horse of Kraljevic Marko, while the Turks are convinced that they were made by the winged charger of Djerzelez Alija. Myths and memories overlap and patterns emerge between them.

They did not even squabble about all this, so convinced were both sides in their own belief. And, there was never an instance of any one of them being able to convince another, nor that any one had changed his belief.[13]

This is a salutary reminder that although human beings do participate in a corporate 'Great Memory', the memories of nations and tribes can be manipulated or misused. Sometimes overlapping memories are simply irreconcilable.

To return to Kosovo briefly, throughout the recent conflict the Decani Monastery provided sanctuary for dispossessed Kosovar Albanians, Serbs and Gypsies. It is the home of Fr Sava, a young monk whose website has earned him the nickname of 'cybermonk'. Throughout the conflict he has used the power of new technology to disseminate a message of peace and reconciliation and has not flinched from being critical both of the Belgrade regime and even of his own Church. And yet, within the ancient monastery church with its gorgeous frescoes there is a huge corona or chandelier forged from swords from the Battle of Kosovo in 1389 when Prince Lazar rode onto the Blackbird Field in order, so some would say, to defend Christian Europe from the forces of Islam. Fr Sava speaks of his fears and of the future. 'We must learn to let go of our history,' he says, 'and perhaps a few of our memories.'

The Elusive Memory?

If remembering becomes solely constitutive of tribal and ethnic identity all too easily it becomes the tinder out of which spring the destructive flames of nationalism. David Jones stimulates his readers, and those who look at his paintings, to an understanding of memory and the myth interpreted as coterminous with all human sign-making and artistic endeavour. This is a vision which properly puts God at the centre and derives all that is human from that divine condescension. Johan

Huizinga, exploring the perceptions at the end of another era, suggests that: 'Every age yearns for a more beautiful world. The deeper the desperation about the confusing present, the more intense the yearning.'[14]

Though he, of course, was writing about the late medieval period in the Low Countries it is no less true for us at beginning of the twenty-first century. As the poet Geoffrey Hill asks in one of his recent poems, 'what is to become of memory?'[15]

And yet, while I think that there are serious matters to be addressed, as our society's valuing of memory becomes elusive and slippery, I am not inclined to be quite as pessimistic as either Hill or David Jones. While it is easy to be seduced into thinking that the modern technological age has brought with it a more mono-chrome civilization I do not believe that to be the case. Neither do I believe the past deposits of memory are being progressively undervalued. We are rightly morally outraged at death, destruction and displaced refugees in the Balkans but for all that we are probably better placed to understand the complex forces which have brought this about. David Jones would be the first to admit that the deposits of corporate memory that make up Britishness, for example, are a result of tides of migration. What enrichment of memory will be possible in the future as we learn to value that which has been brought to us by our African, Caribbean and Asian citizens?

However, George Steiner's intuition that David Jones will prove to be the poet for the twenty-first century may yet prove itself to be true. We may find it possible

to reclaim the territory of myth and memory and
humanize the machine. And so I end with a moment of
questioning silence from *In Parenthesis*: the scene of the
battle at Mametz's Wood in 1915 where many members
of David Jones's platoon lie dead and are visited by the
Queen of the Woods who brings them flowers:

> The Queen of the Woods has cut bright boughs of
>   various flowering.
>   These knew her influential eyes. Her awarding
> hands can pluck for each their fragile prize.
>   She speaks to them according to precedence.
>   She knows what's due to this elect society. She
> can choose twelve gentle-men. She knows who is
> most lord between the high trees and on the
> open down.
>   Some she gives white berries
>   some she gives brown
> Emil has a curious crown it's
>   made of golden saxifrage.
> Fatty wears sweet-briar,
> he will reign with her for a thousand years.
>   For Balder she reaches high to fetch his.
>   Ulrich smiles for his myrtle wand.
>   That swine Lillywhite has daisies to his chain –
> you'd hard-ly credit it.
>   She plaits torques of equal splendour for Mr
> Jenkins and Billy Crower.
>   Hansel with Gronwy share dog-violets for a
> palm, where they lie in serious embrace beneath
> the twisted tripod.

Siôn gets St John's Wort – that's fair enough.
Dai Great-coat, she can't find him anywhere –
she calls
Both high and low, she had a very special one for him.
Among this July noblesse she is mindful of
December wood – when the trees of the forest
beat against each other because of him.
She carries to Aneirin-in-the-nullah a rowan
spring, for the Glory of Guenedota. You
couldn't hear what she said to him, because she
was careful for the Disciplines of the Wars.[16]

Notes

1. David Jones, *In Parenthesis* (London: Faber & Faber, 1937), p. xv.
2. Jones, *In Parenthesis*, p. 13.
3. Jones, *In Parenthesis*, p. 73.
4. George Steiner, *The Death of Tragedy* (London: Faber & Faber, 1961), p. 323.
5. David Jones, 'The Myth of Arthur', in his *Epoch and Artist* (London: Faber & Faber, 1959), p. 243.
6. Jones, *In Parenthesis*, pp. 79ff.
7. David Jones, 'Art and Sacrament', in *Epoch and Artist*, p. 157.
8. Jones, 'Art and Sacrament', in *Epoch and Artist*, p. 175.
9. Rowan Williams, *On Christian Theology* (Oxford: Basil Blackwell, 2000), p. 199.
10. Dom Gregory Dix, *The Shape of the Liturgy* (London: A. & C. Black, 1945), p. 744.
11. David Jones, *The Anathemata* (London: Faber & Faber, 1952), p. 49.
12. David Jones, *The Sleeping Lord* (London: Faber & Faber, 1974), p. 9.

13. Ivo Andric, *The Bridge over the Drina* (London: The Harvill Press, 1995), p. 17.
14. Johan Huizinga, *The Autumn of the Middle Ages* (Chicago: Irons Payton & Mammitzch, 1996), p. 30.
15. Geoffrey Hill, *The Triumph of Love* (Harmondsworth: Penguin Books, 1998), pp. 74–75.
16. Jones, *In Parenthesis*, pp. 185–87.

Aftermath

RONALD BLYTHE

A flood of wonderful stories followed the disturbing silence of the desert and preceded Christ's first sermon in his home synagogue, where his voice had not been heard before. He had read an enchanting passage from Isaiah which begins 'The Spirit of the Lord God is upon me' (chapter 61), but he had soon checked the pleasure which the beautiful language and his own arresting voice was giving to the congregation by a harsh attack on those who enjoyed the eloquence of prophets but ignored their commands. Such criticism was too much for those who only minutes before had 'wondered at the gracious words' of the young speaker, and they ran him out of town.

I have often fancifully believed that Jesus' first words in church from a passage which everyone present would have known by heart, but which he made sound thrillingly new, set the standard for Christianity's complex relationship with the great literature it has inspired. The Word itself was taught in masterly words, first by Paul before the Gospels themselves were written, but these words were taught originally by someone who wrote nothing down other than a sentence in the dust. And yet Christ's storytelling, his history-teaching and oratory, his heard words, cohere with Paul's outpouring of letters to create a literary masterpiece which has been the muse of every kind of writer ever since. Even those bemused by the Church's claims, and in this book we have an agnostic and an atheist, are strangely empowered by what they fret against. For in order to unbelieve they have to read the Old and New Testaments, and here they come into close contact with themselves at two impressionably literary levels: first, as children listening to Luke's account of the Nativity, for example; secondly, as professional writers faced with such a parade of literary excellence – the psalms, Job, the parables, Romans – that they are forced to revere this if nothing else. Also, as has been acknowledged, nearly all the best authors of the Western world weigh in over the centuries and say, 'Do not take us for credulous creatures or for that matter brilliant embroiderers of a sacred myth, or simply writers of our time.'

Neither doubter nor dismisser, if they happen to be good writers, are able to leave the subject alone – which one imagines they could have done if it was not so gloriously set out on the page. A. N. Wilson rises to Hazlittian heights in his condemnation of the new liturgies.

Responses such as these are a necessity for the Church. Here we have four people being required to explain as openly as they can their debt to a great Christ-haunted literature which began its long and inescapable history when its inspirer was still walking the earth. If 'Christianity' was withdrawn from the Eng. Lit. shelves, what would be left? And if we do not know the Scriptures and all that stems from them in Europe's 2000 years of at first underground and then dominant Christ-based writings, how can we know anything, culturally speaking?

The pace and style and imaginative possibilities of the Faith when put to the pen was clearly evident from the word go. The clergy at various times did all they could to see that these wayward streams of poetry and prose joined the safe river of orthodoxy but, as any anthology will tell you, it was hopeless. St Augustine excepted, we are now far more likely to look for holy certainties in poetry than in the Fathers. Portraits of the latter were painted on the lower panels of the rood-screen, just behind the pulpit – there are some in St Edmund's, Southwold – and I have often thought of some less than learned mediaeval priest blushing to be in their company as he held forth. I think, too, of the voices of those named in the Incumbents' Board, and how they sounded in the aisles as the English language developed. It was Latin behind the screen and English before it. Strict liturgy in the chancel and moralizing tales in the nave. The mystery of the one and the raciness of the other set many a budding author off. The marriage of symbols and narration brought forth plays, verse, 'fiction' and a theology which fed English literature – and vice versa – for centuries. Thomas Hardy did not choose to point his work in a similar way to the punctuation of the *Book of Common Prayer* because in a sense he had no choice. Those masterly inflections were in him and could not be avoided. But now and then he would make his villagers reveal themselves as unlettered Christians stumbling about in a whirl of words which were holy enough – but what did they mean? He makes Joseph Poorgrass in *Far from the Madding Crowd* articulate these words in what the farmworker calls 'my scripture manner, which is my second nature'.[1]

David Scott's essay opens with Bede's account of Caedmon's second nature, thrust from sight though it was by his own belief that such a way with words was not for the likes of him. Possibly he shrank, not from singing but from the kind of songs which accompanied drinking, as David Scott says. Scholars now shrink from the charming picture of a simple man toiling on a monastic farm giving sudden vent to a marvellous *Hymn* due to a dream. They recognize this *Hymn* as the first known usage of a traditional pagan poetic form for a Christian purpose. The earliest denial we have that the devil should have the best tunes. From Caedmon's *Hymn* there descended *Beowulf* and *Piers Plowman* – and even John Masefield's *The Everlasting Mercy*. The coming of Christ into northern Europe chased away the acceptance of meaningless fate. It was the arrival of hope and the routing of something which these everlastingly warring German tribes dubbed *Wyrd*, or a dull inevitability from which only courage in battle might possibly rescue you. Caedmon's *Hymn* invites us to acknowledge both creation and the Creator. Seven hundred years later, William Langland, seeing England decimated by the Black Death, would bring everyone who remained to a field in Herefordshire, make Christ a ploughman and his worship to take place in a barn. I am sorry that

Ronald Blythe

neither Caedmon's *Hymn* nor lines from *Piers Plowman* can be found in the hymnbooks. As David Scott remarks, 'The Church could be more of a midwife for poetry'. Our finest hymns are by good, and often, great poets but neither their names nor those of the composers who set them are given on *Songs of Praise* (the television programme which, more than any other agency, is re-teaching the hymnbook). The approach is more emotional than intellectual.

'What is a hymn?' someone asked St Augustine. His reply was: 'A hymn is the praise of God by singing. A hymn is a song embodying the praise of God. If there be merely praise but not praise of God, it is not a hymn. If there be praise, and praise of God but not sung, it is not a hymn. For it to be a hymn it is needful, therefore, for it to have three things – praise, praise of God and these sung.'[2] I imagine that St Augustine had been instructed by his friend St Ambrose, Bishop of Milan, who insisted upon congregational singing and who wrote the lovely 'Come, thou Redeemer of the Earth' and the Caedmonian 'Creator of the Earth and Sky'.

David Scott describes the subversive nature of the parson-poet with an acute understanding of his role in the Church. Gerard Manley Hopkins had moved from the poetry-tolerant Church of England to the Jesuits and had to sign up to the Spiritual Exercises of St Ignatius, one of which was the following:

One must grow cold to all things: love of friends, country, parents; particular interests; kinds of learning . . . In fine, the ideal put forward is that of a soldier held by no tie of affection ... utterly detached from all natural desire ... The beautiful things that grow ... human love with its impulses; music, dance and song; the conquering of nature; art and dreams; have no value in themselves, and must be bartered for whatever helps piety.[3]

Suffice to add that it would have been impossible for anyone with but a fragment of Hopkins's personality and literary genius to 'grow cold' to anything contained in this list. His helpless disobedience would, eventually, fire the Church. Hopkins's prose alone – he kept ravishingly beautiful nature notes and was a master when it came to writing about weather – is a denial of the religious asceticism of his order. His work is a famous example of a God-given gift manifesting itself at the last, and of what the Church owes to its poets.

George Herbert is, of course, Anglicanism's perfect voice. It remains a difficult voice for all its apparent simplicity; its Christianity so compressed and shaped into the poetic conceits of the early seventeenth century that we most likely sing his hymns with more sense of their beauty than of their meaning. Maybe this does not matter. His 'something understood' persists. Now and then I enjoy unlocking one of his 'cabinets' to let the village choir see inside, for example, the one which says:

> A man that looks on glass,
>   On it may stay his eye;
> Or if he pleaseth, through it pass,
>   And then the heaven espy.[4]

Herbert saw the last of the mediaeval glass, before the
second 'cleansing' of the churches by the Puritans broke
it down, and knew its purpose (to carry the gaze via art
to the eternal), although it was admissible simply to
enjoy the picture. Like Hopkins, he relied on an inter-
mediary to publish his poems – his old Cambridge
friend, Nicholas Ferrar. Unlike Hopkins, he did not have
to wait long for his readership. Sent by Ferrar to the
best Cambridge bookbinder and entitled by him *The
Temple*, Herbert's poetry was an immediate success, and
it continues to filter through English religious consciousness like mercury to this day. It is spare but intellectual,
homely yet magnificent, complicated yet not too hard
to get the gist of.

Our living Herbert is another Welshman, R. S.
Thomas. His is a concise bitterness at times but with
astonishing visionary joys. He is able to put his finger
on those things which trouble a priest or a country parson. He doesn't pretend to love his fellow men. Christian
charity in the good-natured sense which is supposed to
fill the vicarage or rectory is anathema to him. He is
austere and sees past all this. He is unflinchingly truthful
when it comes to looking at himself in the vestry, or at
the altar-rail when everyone else has left. He is continu-
ously self-testing, self-interrogating, and the reader, particularly the parson-reader, might exclaim that there is
nought here for his comfort. And then, as with George
Herbert only with a quite different voice, Christ's own
sweetness of language is heard – a few unforgettable
words. Thomas does not pretend to like his flock. His
first parishioners were as mean as hell and he hasn't a

good word for them. They stand for a type which remains constant still in many a parish and he has set their hypocrisies in his own stoniness. What moves us most about R. S. Thomas is his being able to stare himself in the face, like Rembrandt, and to say what he is looking at. His dread, maybe, is to find that he is like that old priest of Shiloh who presided where there was no open vision. Every priest should read Thomas. He is often able to say what some of them would not dare to think. Churchgoers too should be brave enough to have an uncomfortable time with him. His clarity is intensely moving.

There is no sign – rather the reverse – that the sacred has lost its appeal where the poet is concerned. There *is* an 'after Geoffrey Hill' – James Harpur, for instance. His richly dark 'Magna Karistia' acts as a brake to the fatuities with which we marked the Christian calendar as the year AD 2000 dawned. This fine, tragic poem was inspired by a mediaeval friar and it reminded me of the indebtedness of so many of today's religious poets to the writings of the English mystics: Clifton Wolter's wonderful translation of the anonymous *The Cloud of Unknowing* and of Richard Rolle's *The Fire of Love*, and most of all his translation of Julian of Norwich's *Revelations of Divine Love*. Two women in particular, Evelyn Underhill and Helen Waddell, released into the modern world the literary thinking of the Middle Ages. It complemented that of John Mason Neale, Gerard Moultrie and other Victorians who brought the mighty pre-Reformation hymns to light. Even botanies like Richard Mabey's *Flora Britannica*, with their enthralling

Ronald Blythe

history of Christianized plants, offer endless grist to contemporary poetry. Every generation brings to the Church its most fitting – and its rubbish. So it has ever been. The lasting and the soon vanishing. So, sursum corda!

A. N. Wilson thinks that the implications of the modernist crisis in the Catholic Church are a draining away of all belief for any educated twenty-first-century person who, like himself, clung to a vestigial Christianity because of its peerless language. One might doubt the Resurrection but never the transcendent language of *The Book of Common Prayer* and the *King James Bible*, the Tridentine Mass and the culture which until only the other day flowed so inspiringly from this holy literature. And to think that it was the Church itself, and not its enemies, who cut off this flow! Thus he takes it to task, and with relish, being a great man for a fight. He is torn between wondering why writers he admires, such as Dorothy L. Sayers, Rose Macaulay, Barbara Pym and others, having gone so far in doubt, could not have freed themselves altogether from Christ and have recognized his cult at its best as a civilizing force created by the literary masterpieces on which it was founded. Wilson is rightly furious that so many people who are 50 and under are biblically illiterate. A friend of mine took her 16-year-old grandson round King's College, Cambridge, and he was unable to identify the characters in the windows and did not know their tales. Wilson says that the clergy themselves have vandalized and destroyed the loveliest thing that they had inherited from the saints and prophets, poets and scholars, and thus from God, which was the Word put into matchless words. All gone, all gone, put an end to, they say, by Catholics and Protestants alike. The obvious question is, why does he care? Has he not spent a lot of his time dismissing this religion? His answer is cultural. Would one replace Bach's or Handel's librettos with what is read in church this Sunday?

I suppose that each of us has the bit we can't stand, the sentence we jib at. I miss more than I can say those profound sentences which accompanied the giving of the sacraments, those words which went with the very same cup which is their contemporary. 'The blood of Christ,' I murmur – and, silently, 'The blood of our Lord Jesus Christ, which was shed for thee, preserve thy body and soul unto everlasting life. Drink this in remembrance that Christ's blood was shed for thee, and be thankful.' Workworn hands, young hands, shaking hands, a child's hands, and a few vague Amens. A merit of the longer words was that they did not hurry the bread and wine together, but there was much objection to them when the cup was new.

A. N. Wilson weighs into the Church's latest new words with all his literary might, which is considerable. He is surprised to find himself so upset by these changes and feels that he is speaking up for those without a voice in these matters and for those who have a tongue but who haven't used it. Also he has a gift for invective and here is a subject on which he can display it to the full. He allows it to carry him away. 'Islam, the only viable religion of the future.' 'Christian literature . . . came to an end with the generation of T. S. Eliot.' There was a

time when they would have had him out of the Cathedral
and into the nearby Lollards' pit – as indeed they might
have had Mother Julian from up the road, were they
cognisant of her book, which was well written, of
course.

The views of the agnostic Penelope Lively are more
moderate, though penetrating nevertheless. Her quiet-
ness reminds us that the novelist spends all of her or his
working days in a special state of aloneness which has
to be filled with invented people who are themselves
created out of individuals who have been observed by
the writer, either in the present or the past. She says
that she has to impose order and create structure for
these men and women of her imagination, and that they
have to be a fictional reflection of the real world which
has to illuminate and entertain.

'"Only a novel" ... in short, only some work in
which the greatest powers of the mind are displayed, in
which the most thorough knowledge of human nature,
the happiest delineation of its varieties, the liveliest
effusions of wit and humour are conveyed to the world
in the best chosen language', but she rightly says as
much in today's terms. Not so long ago there was talk
of the 'death of the novel' just as there was of the 'death
of God'. Those who said such things liked conclusions
and new beginnings, not understanding that there are
some aspects of creation, divine and human, upon which
the door can never be closed; opened wider, certainly,
narrowed to a chink, frequently – but not shut away
for good or bad. Penelope Lively shows novels and short
stories constantly being born anew, and without their

predecessors having to die in order that they should live. Good fiction has its dates but does not become dated. Not that I always dismiss some less than classic novel which speaks of the 1930s or the 1890s – rather the opposite. The other day found me cheerfully engrossed in a sensational Victorian novel called *Moths* by Ouida which fell out of the bookcase when I was searching for Henry James. Penelope Lively says that she should be speculating about the future of the book (which is a polite way of anticipating its death) but instead she is pleased to see that it is doing nicely. She quotes the Director of the British Library on the book. It was, he said, 'the most lasting and efficient information device going: portable, user-friendly, not dependent on any external support system'.

She herself describes fiction as the most mutable of literary forms which is re-worked by each generation of novelists. She draws the line between fiction as popular entertainment and what is sometimes called the literary novel, though without condemnation of the former. But she rightly insists on our need of serious fiction to take us forward philosophically and ethically. The pleasure principle is for me never more evident than when I am reading certain novels. To turn the television off and to pick up an old favourite or a new fictional experience – what happiness! To open the page at the marker, to lose oneself in fresh chapters – what contentment! To be honest, I have never much liked fictionalized Catholicism, unless it is Willa Cather's *Death Comes for the Archbishop* or something equally superb. Nor have I ever much enjoyed fictionalized Anglicanism outside

Trollope or Barbara Pym. For centuries Christian fiction was expressed in allegory, its great 'novels' being the work of Dante and Bunyan, Chaucer and Langland. A miraculous development of this writing during the eighteenth century created the novel form which pre-occupies most readers today. There is nothing which cannot be said in a novel. Fiction teaches us the facts of life. Its narrative power, as strong as river currents, bears us along. The teachings of Christ, though rarely specified, are frequently retaught by novelists.

Richard Marsh's 'David Jones and the Elusive Memory' touched me deeply. This was familiar ground. At first the writers and artists of the Great War floundered in its religion-turned-to-mud, not knowing what to make of all that they had been told to believe in being brought so low. But, eventually, the human spirit being what it is, an essence of its Maker, each individual possessor of it found a personal interpretation of the trenches. My teenage father fought at Gallipoli, my old friend John Nash painted both the Somme and the Second World War battles, as did his brother Paul (the latter's pictures of aerial warfare deserving of Yeats' phrase 'terrible beauty'), thus both these conflicts coming close to home. Richard Marsh saw Kosovo, saw what David Jones had seen elsewhere, for as anyone listening to the news on any day these days will have heard, the hard facts are the same. People are massacred, cities are wrecked, women are raped, children are orphaned, economies are ruined and, at the end, nothing was worth it. The war. David Jones, the artist-poet, went out into the no-man's-land of faith which lay scattered across Europe like one of Paul Nash's splintered trees and worked his way back to God via certain enduring myths which had served both Catholicism and humankind's love of stories from the Celts on. In his common language autobiographies *In Parenthesis* and *The Anathemata*, the division between prose and poetry remained blurred. One thinks of William Blake or St John of the Cross and of James Joyce. Central to Jones's vision and eccentric commentary are his reflections on 'Art and Sacrament' which one reader has called 'the best account in English of sacramental theology'. Poets were originally required to be the tribe's remembrancers. Richard Marsh's thoughtful and, in so many ways, privately experienced essay is a restoration of landmarks – a reminder of the way we have come, a pointing-out of its signs.

Notes

1. Thomas Hardy, *Far from the Madding Crowd* (London: Macmillan, 1968), p. 464.
2. St Augustine, *Expositions on the Book of Psalms* (Psalm 73).
3. From St Ignatius of Loyola's *Spiritual Exercises* (1541), in Norman White, *Hopkins: A Literary Biography* (Oxford: Clarendon Press, 1992), p. 87.
4. George Herbert, 'The Elixir', in *The English Poems of George Herbert* (London: J. M. Dent, 1974), p. 188.